FEMINISM

The March Toward Equal Rights for Women

Jill Dearman

Illustrated by Alexis Cornell

Nomad Press
A division of Nomad Communications
10 9 8 7 6 5 4 3 2 1

This book was manufactured by Versa Press,
East Peoria, Illinois
April 2019, Job #J18-13159

ISBN Softcover: 978-1-61930-755-1
ISBN Hardcover: 978-1-61930-752-0

Educational Consultant, Marla Conn

Questions regarding the ordering of this book should be addressed to
Nomad Press
2456 Christian St.
White River Junction, VT 05001
www.nomadpress.net

Titles in the Inquire & Investigate
Social Issues of the Twentieth Century set

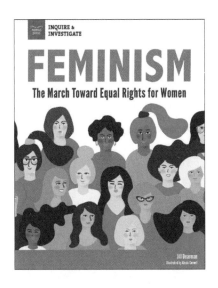

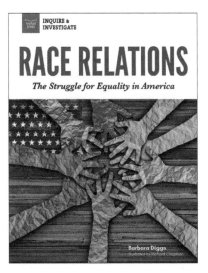

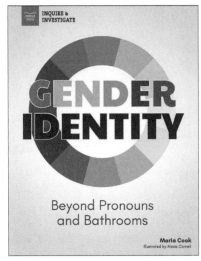

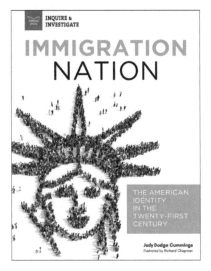

To Holly Dearman-Kastor
With thanks to Lorna Gottesman and Paisley Currah

Interested in primary sources?

Look for this icon.

You can use a smartphone or tablet app to scan the QR codes and explore more! Cover up neighboring QR codes to make sure you're scanning the right one. You can find a list of URLs on the Resources page.

If the QR code doesn't work, try searching the internet with the Keyword Prompts to find other helpful sources.

 feminism

What are source notes?

In this book, you'll find small numbers at the end of some paragraphs. These numbers indicate that you can find source notes for that section in the back of the book. Source notes tell readers where the writer got their information. This might be a news article, a book, or another kind of media. Source notes are a way to know that what you are reading is information that other people have verified. They can also lead you to more places where you can explore a topic that you're curious about!

Contents

TIMELINE

1839 .... Mississippi grants women the right to hold property in their own name, with their husband's permission. It is the first state to give women this right.

1848 .... At Seneca Falls, New York, 300 women and men sign the Declaration of Sentiments, a plea for the end of discrimination against women in all spheres of society.

1869 .... The first woman suffrage law in the United States is passed, in the territory of Wyoming.

1890 .... Wyoming grants women the right to vote in all elections. It is the first state to give women this right.

1900 .... By now, every state has passed legislation modeled after New York's Married Women's Property Act (1848), granting married women some control over their property and earnings.

1916 .... Margaret Sanger tests the validity of New York's anti-contraception law by establishing a clinic in Brooklyn. The most well-known of birth control advocates, she is one of hundreds arrested during a 40-year period for working to establish women's right to control their own bodies.

1920 .... The Nineteenth Amendment to the U.S. Constitution is ratified. It declares: "The right of citizens of the United States to vote shall not be denied or abridged by the United States or by any State on account of sex."

1963 .... The Equal Pay Act is passed by the U.S. Congress, promising equitable wages for the same work, regardless of the race, color, religion, national origin, or sex of the worker.

1964 .... Title VII of the Civil Rights Act passes. It includes a prohibition against employment discrimination on the basis of race, color, religion, national origin, or sex.

1973 .... *Roe v. Wade*, 410 U.S. 113, and *Doe v. Bolton*, 410 U.S. 179: The U.S. Supreme Court declares that the Constitution protects a woman's right to terminate an early pregnancy, thus making abortion legal in the United States.

1978................................ The Pregnancy Discrimination Act bans employment discrimination against pregnant women.

1981................................ *Kirchberg v. Feenstra*, 450 U.S. 455, 459-60: The U.S. Supreme Court overturns state laws designating a husband "head and master" with unilateral control of property owned jointly with his wife.

1981................................ Sandra Day O'Connor is appointed by President Ronald Reagan to serve as the first woman on the Supreme Court.

2005................................ Hillary Rodham Clinton becomes the first former First Lady to be elected to public office, as a U.S. senator from New York. Condoleezza Rice becomes the first black, female U.S. secretary of state.

2007................................ Nancy Pelosi becomes the first female speaker of the U.S. House of Representatives.

2009................................ Sonia Sotomayor is nominated as the 111th U.S. Supreme Court justice. She becomes the first Hispanic American and the third woman to serve.

2010................................ The Affordable Health Care Act is signed into law. Under this law, private health insurance companies must provide birth control without co-pays or deductibles. The law requires private insurance companies to cover preventive services.

2013................................ The ban against women in military combat positions is removed; this overturned a 1994 Pentagon decision restricting women from combat roles.

2013................................ *United States v. Windsor 570*: The U.S. Supreme Court decides that the law that restricts federal recognition of same-sex marriage is unconstitutional because it violates the equal protection clause of the Constitution.

2016................................ Hillary Clinton becomes the first woman to be nominated for president by a major political party when she receives the Democratic Party's presidential nomination.

Introduction

What Is Feminism?

WE'VE BEEN FIGHTING FOR A LONG TIME.

How has feminism changed from the first wave to now?

IT SURE FEELS LIKE IT, BUT IT'S ONLY BEEN 100 YEARS SINCE WE WON THE RIGHT TO VOTE!

THE VOTE WAS JUST THE START— WE FOUND OUR VOICES QUICKLY.

YEAH?

THE FIRST WAVE BEGAN WITH SILENCE, AND NOW SO MANY VOICES ARE BEING HEARD!

As the awareness and needs of a society change and develop, feminism evolves as a way to seek out answers and develop systems that promote equality for all.

Do you think men and women are equal? Do you think they enjoy the same rights and privileges around the world? What about jobs—can men and women work the same jobs and get paid the same for their work?

Many people would say yes, all people should be treated equally, whether they're male, female, or gender nonconforming. But the way our world works doesn't always reflect this ideal of equality. Women are often treated differently from men. Even today, in the United States, women statistically earn less than men working the same jobs. You'll find few women heading up large corporations. And women are more likely than men to live in poverty.

Women have, however, come a long way in many parts of the world. In the United States, for example, women couldn't even vote before 1919! Now, women can be found at almost all levels of the U.S. government.

While feminism has existed in different ways since humans began recording history, what we now call the first wave of feminism centered around the struggle to gain the right to vote. And a key player in this struggle was a woman named Alice Paul (1885–1977).

THE SILENT SENTINELS

Alice Paul believed that all humans were obligated to leave the world a better place than they found it. Born in Mount Laurel, New Jersey, and raised in the Quaker tradition, Alice was determined to carry out that belief by working toward equality for all.

As a Quaker, Alice was deeply influenced by the practice of "silent meeting." In her Quaker meeting house, attendees would gather and sit in pews, as in a Christian church. Instead of being led in a sermon, Quakers sat in silence, and an individual could speak if they wanted to. But talking was not expected, and it was understood that speech should be meaningful, not merely superficial.

Mrs. W.L. Prendergast, Mrs. W.L. Colt, Doris Stevens, and Alice Paul

credit: Library of Congress

It was in this spirit that Alice Paul led a group of women in the newly formed National Women's Party (NWP) in 1917. Their goal was to obtain the right to vote for women. On January 9, they met with Woodrow Wilson (1856–1924), the 28th president of the United States, but did not find an enthusiastic ally in him. President Wilson advised them to rally public support if they wanted his endorsement for the vote. The NWP members strategized and then made a decision.

The very next day, they picketed outside the White House. The women were soon nicknamed the "Silent Sentinels," because they stood like guards outside the White House gates, never speaking. Their messages were conveyed through picket signs instead of spoken words.

Alice Paul was clear that even when criticized directly, the members of the group should not reply—instead, they simply stood and held their ground in silence. Identified by the signature colors they wore—purple, white, and gold—they believed in a singular message: equal rights for women, beginning with the vote.

Learn more about Alice Paul and hear first-hand accounts of how women were treated in prison in this video. How do you think the public reacted to these images?

Alice Stokes Paul video

Silent Sentinels on the picket line, 1917

credit: Library of Congress

FEMINISM | INTRODUCTION

Alison Turnbull Hopkins pickets at the White House on New Jersey Day.

credit: Library of Congress

MR. PRESIDENT HOW LONG MUST WOMEN WAIT FOR LIBERTY

The authorities began to turn against them. Beginning in June 1917, suffrage protestors were arrested, stripped, and forced to submit to inhumane treatment at the Occoquan Workhouse in the District of Columbia. This went on six days a week.

Alice Paul was arrested on October 20, 1917, and while in prison, she went on a hunger strike. This was another way for them to protest. Many women refused to eat and were force-fed. The escalating standoff between the imprisoned women and the workhouse employees, who were all men, finally erupted on November 14 in what became known as the "Night of Terror."

On that night, W.H. Whittaker, superintendent of the Occoquan Workhouse, ordered the brutal beatings of the female prisoners. They were punched, kicked, slammed into floors and walls, and choked.

FEMINIST FACT

The word *feminism* didn't come into popular usage until the 1960s and 1970s, during what is known as the second wave of feminism. As with most aspects of feminism, people disagree about the term's origins. It is generally accepted that the word stems from the French word *feminisme*, a term coined in 1837 by French philosopher Charles Fourier (1772–1837).

"There will never be a new world order until women are a part of it."
—Alice Paul

FEMINIST FACT

The United States still operates as a patriarchal society. The word *patriarchy* stems from the Greek word *patriarkhia*, meaning "system of society or government by fathers or elder males of the community." The word was first recorded in the 1630s. In this system, men have more power than women.

Lucy Burns (1879–1966), one of the prisoners, was handcuffed to the cell's bars with her hands above her head and left there all night. Other women stood with their arms raised above their heads in support of Lucy until she was released.

Once word got out to the public about the brutal treatment of the suffragists, public support of women's right to vote began to grow.

Finally, in 1920, the 19th Amendment to the Constitution was passed, granting women the right to vote. Alice Paul then moved on to her next mission of adding an equal rights amendment to the U.S. Constitution.

Suffragist Kate Heffelfinger after her release from Occoquan Prison, c. 1917

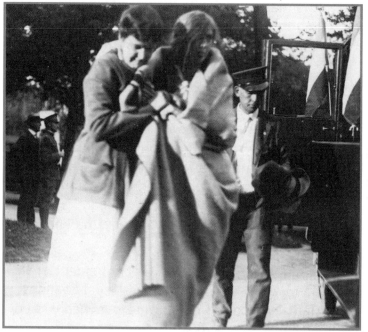

credit: Library of Congress

WAVES OF FEMINISM

There is no one definition of feminism, but rather an overarching goal: to establish political, social, and economic equality between the sexes. As the struggles of Alice Paul and the other suffragists show, feminism is a series of movements in response to the inequalities of the time.

Throughout history there have been several waves of feminism in America. Let's take a look at them.

First Wave: The Right to Vote First-wave feminism refers to the period in the late nineteenth and early twentieth century when women fought to obtain the right to vote. This was called the Suffrage Movement. First-wave feminism was not limited to this one issue, though. It was also a time of social awakening, when people worked to change some of the social issues they saw, such as improving the lives of the poor and sick.

Second Wave: The Awakening Second-wave feminism refers generally to the period between the early 1960s and early 1980s, a tumultuous time in American history in general and for women in particular. In the 1960s, married women began to form what were called consciousness-raising groups, where they could share their experiences of marriage and parenthood and discuss issues they felt were important. The following decade saw issues such as birth control, daycare for children, and equal pay for women come to the forefront.

Perhaps the most prominent aspect of feminism during this second wave was the issue of abortion. The 1973 court case *Roe v. Wade* said that laws that criminalized abortions, as well as limited access to them, were unconstitutional. People are still discussing and arguing about abortion today.

GLASS CEILINGS

In June 2008, former First Lady and U.S. Senator Hillary Rodham Clinton (1947–) spoke these words in her concession speech after losing the Democratic nomination for president to Barack Obama.

"Although we weren't able to shatter that highest, hardest glass ceiling this time, thanks to you, it's got about 18 million cracks in it, and the light is shining through like never before, filling us all with the hope and the sure knowledge that the path will be a little easier next time."[2]

In November 2016, Clinton, who had gone on to serve President Obama as secretary of state, gave a variation of the "cracks in the glass ceiling" speech in her concession speech to Donald J. Trump, whom she ran against for president. In the history of the United States, there has never been a female president or vice president.

The acronym **LGBTQ** stands for lesbian, gay, bisexual, transgender, and queer or questioning.

Third Wave: Intersectionality This period of feminism blossomed in the 1990s and lasted until approximately 2012. The focus of this era was on the many different forms of oppression women face that are not based on gender. This is called intersectionality, and it's the way different forms of discrimination combine and intersect. Race, class, and sexual orientation were all areas of focus for third-wave feminists. During this era, many women of color, lower-income women, and LGBTQ people began to speak up more forcefully about how they'd felt left out from early feminist movements.

FEMINISM TODAY?

Do we still need feminism in a world where women can vote, work at the same jobs as men, and make their own decisions? What are people fighting for? Sadly, there are still injustices against women. Sexual harassment, pay inequity, and the changing of laws that protect women all mean that feminism is still extremely important in today's world.

A women's march in 2017

credit: Fibonacci Blue (CC BY 2.0)

Some people believe that we are currently experiencing a strong backlash against the progress women have made during the last century. One example of this can be found in the story of the Equal Rights Amendment (ERA). This is a proposal that states that the rights guaranteed by the Constitution apply equally to all persons regardless of their sex. In 1923, three years after women attained the right to vote, Alice Paul introduced the ERA as the next step in bringing "equal justice under law" to all citizens.

It took about half a century for Congress to send it to the states for ratification in 1972. Ten years later, even with an extended time limit granted by Congress, the ERA had been ratified by only 37 states—that's three states short of the required number to write it into the Constitution. To this day, the battle continues.

In some countries, the situation can be worse, even dangerous. Women can be treated unfairly and even brutally with no way of escaping. Girls are not allowed to go to school and get an education. Girls are married at extremely young ages with no choice in the matter.

> There is still a long way to go before women are considered equal around the world.

In *Feminism*, we'll learn the history of the American feminist movement, from its ancient European beginnings through the different waves to today's work. You'll meet key leaders of the different movements and travel the world to see how people define feminism and how groups practice intersectionality to gain equality and equity for everyone.

VOCAB LAB

Write down what you think each word means. What root words can you find to help you? What does the context of the word tell you?

equality, **feminism**, **inhumane**, **intersectionality**, **patriarchy**, **picket**, **privilege**, and **suffrage**.

Compare your definitions with those of your friends or classmates. Did you all come up with the same meanings? Turn to the text and glossary if you need help.

KEY QUESTIONS

- **What does the term *feminism* mean to you?**

- **Why did the public pay more attention to the suffrage movement after the Night of Terror?**

- **Who is the most responsible for ensuring all humans have equal rights?**

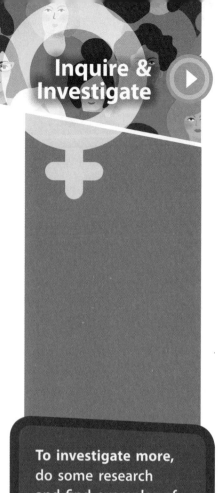

SHARE YOUR CONCERNS

How is the world different for those of different genders? What are some of the different experiences, reactions, and ideas that different genders have? In this activity, you'll share your thoughts in a safe space with people who aren't the same gender as you.

- **Ask a group of classmates or friends to finish this sentence according to their own gender:** Having my gender identity means . . . . Have everyone write down one or two responses on individual sticky notes.

- **On a whiteboard, put the sticky notes in groups according to gender identity.** In those groups, put the sticky notes in positive and negative sections. For example, someone might write, "Being female means getting to wear skirts when it's hot" or "Being male means not letting yourself cry."

- **As a group, discuss the idea on each sticky note.** Consider these questions.

  - Can a male, female, or nonconforming gender do this? Why or why not?

  - Do people of all genders want to do this? What's preventing them?

  - Has this action been open to other genders in the past? What changed?

  - How can society support the needs and wishes of all genders?

To investigate more, do some research and find examples of times in history when a woman protested a law that kept her from doing something she wanted to do. For example, women have been barred from working certain jobs and holding office. How did they work to change those laws? How long did it take? How did changing one law change the world for many people?

Chapter 1 ▶
Women's Lives in History

JUST WHAT CAN WE LEARN FROM THE WOMEN IN OUR PAST?

What was life like for women before the suffrage movement began?

NOT A LOT, AS IT TURNS OUT.

WHAT A BUMMER!

IT'S TRUE THAT THERE WASN'T MUCH RECORDED ABOUT WOMEN IN THE PAST.

BUT THERE'S A LOT WE CAN INFER BASED ON WHAT WE DON'T KNOW!

Life was a struggle for many women throughout history. In most countries, women weren't allowed to own property, hold certain jobs, or be part of government.

Think about the history books you've read. Who were the people leading countries, declaring revolutions, defining laws, and overseeing much of daily life? You might have noticed the names that appear most frequently in history books are those of men. Where were the women? What were they doing?

For much of human history, in many areas of the world, men have been the ones to record historical events and ideas, so women have often been left out of descriptions of the past. While we can't travel back in time, what we can do is see what rights women possessed long ago and what contributions they made to society.

We can also take a look at some of the women who had a deep impact on their culture, despite often being considered second-class citizens.

MEET SAPPHO

In ancient Greece, a poet named Sappho lived on the Isle of Lesbos around the seventh and sixth centuries BCE. Sappho wrote lyrical poems about women, poems that are respected and studied to this day.

Sappho was born into a noble family. After marrying and having a child, she became head of a learning academy for unmarried women. Back then, wealthy families used to send their daughters away to be schooled in areas such as social graces, singing, and poetry recitation.

Found on a vase, one of the earliest surviving images of Sappho, from c. 470 BCE

The community that formed on the Isle of Lesbos around Sappho's academy focused on the celebration of women. Religious festivals celebrated the arrival of a girl's first menstrual period. Sappho was a gifted musician and dancer, and led readings and performances that blended many art forms, including poetry. Sappho even used many of her students as subjects.

> Before Sappho, the Greeks wrote a lot of poetry that was about the gods.

For example, *The Odyssey* by Homer describes the journey of one man, Odysseus, trying to return home from the Trojan War. *The Odyssey* is written in the third person—readers know what is going on in the minds of many different characters, instead of having access to only one perspective.

Sappho broke with this tradition and form by writing in the first person from her own perspective.

> Deathless Aphrodite of the spangled mind,
> child of Zeus, who twists lures, I beg you
> do not break with hard pains,
> O lady, my heart
> but come here if ever before
> you caught my voice far off
> and listening left your father's
> golden house and came . . .

Sappho also showed great innovation by refining poetic meter, the rhythm of a poem. Her rhythm was later named "Sapphic meter." It influenced other important poets, including Ovid (43 BCE–17 CE), a Roman poet who lived during the golden and silver ages of Latin literature and is known for writing about love.

Although Sappho's influence on poetry was great and she was admired during her life, as centuries passed, attitudes changed and people turned against her, possibly because she was a lesbian. For example, a nine-volume edition of Sappho's poetry was published in the third century BCE, but religious institutions destroyed most of these works after the fourth century CE because they contained images of lesbians.

While we can see the lasting influence of a woman in the legacy of poetry that Sappho left behind, there were other women making great strides in their roles as queen.

BRITISH RULERS

Before the twentieth century, almost no women were in positions of public power. Men were the rulers—they ran governments and decided on laws. But there are stories of a few unusual women.

Boudicca (also spelled Boadicea), who died around 60 CE, was an ancient British queen who led a revolt against the Romans, who then ruled parts of Britain. When her husband, Prasutagus, died without a male heir, he left his wealth to his daughters and to Roman Emperor Nero, hoping to win protection for his daughters. Instead, the Romans took his kingdom and humiliated his family.

In response, Boudicca led a rebellion against the Romans and burned several cities, including Londinium, now known as London, England. Thousands were killed, but ultimately, the Romans won. Although the site of the final battle and Boudicca's death are unknown, some people believe she poisoned herself to avoid capture.[8]

AN EARLY SUPPORTER

The ancient Greek philosopher Plato (c.427–c.347 BCE) is perhaps the most influential historical figure who supported equality between the sexes. His best-known work is called *The Republic*. In a series of dialogues, he argues that the dog kingdom doesn't distinguish between the roles of male and female dogs. Either sex can stand guard. He believes this same concept should extend to the human species.

"No office should be reserved for a man just because he is a man or for a woman just because she is a woman. All the capabilities with which nature endows us are distributed among men and women alike."

ANNE BOLEYN

King Henry VIII of England wanted a son so badly, he took some dramatic steps to deal with wives who gave birth to daughters or no children—including having two wives beheaded! One of these wives was Anne Boleyn. Henry divorced his first wife, Catherine of Aragon (1485–1536), in order to marry Anne. Divorce was not recognized by the Roman Catholic Church, but Henry went ahead with the marriage and broke with the Catholic Church, appointing himself the head of the Church of England. Although Anne Boleyn was eventually beheaded—as a result of charges of adultery and treason—she had a great influence during her reign as queen. She solidified England's relationship with France and proved herself a natural in diplomacy. While she didn't give birth to a son, her daughter, Elizabeth, became a powerful queen.

Another example of strong female leadership can be found in Queen Elizabeth I of England (1533–1603). She was the ruler of England when it was a major European power in politics, commerce, and the arts. As the daughter of Henry VIII (1491–1547) and Anne Boleyn (c. 1507–1536), she didn't have a great start in life and had numerous obstacles to overcome before she finally became queen of England in 1558. Once she was queen, Elizabeth quickly made it clear she wasn't going to rule in name only.

Elizabeth never married, despite considering many offers of marriage. Some historians believe she avoided marriage to avoid giving up any power.

> Supposedly she said, "I will have here but one mistress and no master."

While Elizabeth took advice from her ministers, she made all the final decisions in state matters. She was also skilled at manipulating factions, and when she believed she was being challenged, she didn't hesitate to show her wrath.

During her long reign, Elizabeth faced many political challenges. For example, for years Elizabeth played a complicated game with Catholic Spain until King Philip II of Spain (1527–1598) assembled an enormous fleet—known as the Spanish Armada—to invade and conquer Protestant England.

In 1558, in one of the most famous naval battles in history, England defeated the Spanish Armada. Many of the Spanish ships were destroyed by storms as they fled back to Spain.[9]

A painting of Queen Elizabeth I at the National Portrait Gallery in London

SCHOOL AND WORK IN THE MIDDLE AGES

Boudicca and Queen Elizabeth are wonderful examples of powerful women, but their paths weren't the usual ones for women throughout history. Let's take a look at what an ordinary life might have looked like.

In Europe during the Middle Ages, few boys and even fewer girls received an education. Girls from wealthy families were sometimes given enough education to help them perform their tasks as wife and mother, but this learning was very limited. Girls from a peasant background had no chance to learn to read and write.

What little education was available came from family members or tutors, or castle, church, and village schools. Convents were another important way a woman could receive an education. Some girls joined convents when very young to get an education before they married, often at the age of 14. Other girls became nuns after receiving their education.

Historically, witch hunts have taken place all around the world, including Europe and America, during many different eras. People, usually women, were accused of performing witchcraft, hunted down, and often executed. People who used herbs and were considered healers were often targeted. In England, mainly poverty-stricken widows and other poor women who did not have the resources to defend themselves were unjustly accused of practicing witchcraft. From 1470 to 1770, the number of executions for witchcraft in Europe totaled a whopping 3,000.[13]

The Salem witch trials took place in Massachusetts in 1692. Read this article to find out what happened. How would you have felt living through those times?

 Nat Geo Kids Salem witches

A convent education typically included reading and writing in Latin, religion, embroidery, weaving, music, and even some medical training to help in the frequent times of war. The most educated nuns became abbesses and were treated as equals by men of their social class. Still, for most girls and women, convents weren't an option. Convents frequently required women to bring a dowry of money or land to help support the convent. How could poor families afford that?

The Protestant movement of the late sixteenth century did little to help the cause of female education. While Protestantism broadened who was given an education, it limited what was taught. Protestants believed that women should be literate enough to read the Bible and maybe teach it to their children—but not much else.

Girls were thought to be feeble-minded and incapable of learning beyond a basic level. Can you imagine if you were never encouraged to learn literature, math, and science?

Much of women's work from the Middle Ages onwards was domestic work, centered around having and raising children, cooking, cleaning, taking care of animals, brewing beer, and spinning wool. Some middle-class women helped their husbands in their trades and occasionally even took over a business after a husband's death. A few ran their own businesses, such as wool spinning or glove making.

The years 1500 to 1800 saw an increase in the number of women who worked as dyers, embroiderers, washerwomen, bakers, midwives, and, very commonly, domestic servants.

Farmers' wives might grow vegetables, raise animals, or make candles or soap that they would sell at markets. All of this in addition to raising children! Wealthy women were also busy, but in a different way. They were organizing households, managing servants, and running estates or businesses while their husbands were away.

WOMEN BRANCH OUT

The European Renaissance (1300s–1600s) was a time of rebirth and renewal, when people became more aware of their connection to each other, to art, to architecture, to the world beyond their own village, and to the potential of science and invention.

During this time, artists such as Leonardo da Vinci (1452–1519) and Michelangelo (1475–1564) created works of art, Gerardus Mercator (1512–1594) made a more reliable map of the world, and Nicolaus Copernicus (1473–1543) proved the earth rotates around the sun and not the other way around!

> Did women experience a renaissance, a period of growth and expansion, along with men?

A small number of women did. Sofonisba Anguissola (1532–1625) was one of the most important portrait artists of the Renaissance. As a woman, Sofonisba was not allowed to study and draw nude models, so she began to paint portraits. Instead of painting people in formal poses, however, she painted them in ordinary settings. She also painted many formal portraits when she was the court painter for the king of Spain for 14 years.

Eleanor of Aquitaine (c. 1122–1204) was perhaps the most powerful woman in twelfth-century Europe. As the daughter of the duke of Aquitaine, she inherited a huge part of France, owning more land than the king of France. As the wife and mother of powerful kings, she was always politically active, often managing the kingdom as well as her own lands. Read more about her long and exceptional life at this website.

 Britannica Eleanor of Aquitaine

As time went on, women found more opportunities available to them. The Industrial Revolution saw the beginning of factory work for women (and children). Factory conditions were often terrible in Britain. The 1847 Factory Act limited women and children to 10 hours a day in textile factories—men worked even longer hours. Women also worked as servants, cleaners, and laundresses. Most working-class women had to work to help support their families.

The inventions of the typewriter in 1868 and telephone in 1876 opened up more jobs for women, such as secretarial work. Professions such as law and medicine were still mostly closed to women.

COLONIAL AMERICA

Let's hop across the pond and see what life was like for women in the New World. During colonial times in America, both boys and girls were taught to read so that they could study the Bible.

A colonial woman spinning wool

credit: from *A Brief History of the United States* by Joel Dorman Steele and Esther Baker Steele, 1885

Girls were usually taught at home or at "dame schools," where women taught reading and writing from their homes. By 1750, 90 percent of women in New England could read and some could write. Boys, on the other hand, were taught both reading and writing because, the thinking went, as they grew older, they would be the ones to handle business transactions.

The ability to read and write and do math would come in handy as more and more women became property owners. In 1771, New York became the first state to require a woman's consent if her husband tried to sell property she brought to the marriage. Also in New York, the Married Woman's Property Act was passed in 1848, allowing married women to own and manage their own property. This became a model for other states to follow.

In addition, the 1862 U.S. Homestead Act did not make gender one of the criteria for homestead ownership—except for married women. Thousands of single, widowed, and divorced women took advantage of this act to move West and acquire up to 160 acres of federal land in their own names.[7]

Can you imagine what that freedom must have felt like?

Enslaved African Americans had no access to education, but in free black communities in the North, some African American women became teachers. Frances E.W. Harper (1825–1911), the daughter of free black parents, was both a teacher and a poet. Despite the lack of formal education available to most African Americans, many learned what they could through families, communities, and the occasional benefactor.

THE BIRTH OF FRANKENSTEIN

English writer Mary Wollstonecraft (1759–1797) was a fierce advocate for the rights of women. In her most famous book, *A Vindication of the Rights of Woman* (1792), she made the case that women were not innately inferior to men, as men had been claiming for centuries. What they lacked was access to education. She was reviled during her life for her unconventional lifestyle, but was later taken up as a symbol of the twentieth-century feminist movement. Mary died 10 days after giving birth to her daughter, Mary Wollstonecraft Godwin, later known as Mary Shelley (1797–1851) and author of the gothic novel *Frankenstein*. This book is still highly popular today and for decades has been taught from a feminist perspective.

Women in America did similar kinds of work to those in Britain. In early colonial times, the goal was survival. After that, women undertook the traditional roles of running a household and raising children. Women were generally married by 20 and had many children. Partly because of high mortality rates, it was normal to have eight children in one family.

Some women worked as seamstresses or kept boarding houses. Others worked in their husband's occupations, such as printmaking or even shipbuilding.

Although most women received just enough education to read the Bible, a few learned more. Anne Bradstreet (c. 1612–1672) was one of the first poets of the American Colonial Era. She was highly educated and well-read. Her poetry covered both religious and personal topics. She did all this while raising eight children and performing the domestic duties required of women at the time!

Mary Rowlandson (c. 1637–c. 1710) was another colonial author. She wrote of her capture by Native Americans in *The Sovereignty and Goodness of God, Together with the Faithfulness of His Promises Displayed: Being a Narrative of the Captivity and Restauration of Mrs. Mary Rowlandson*. This was published multiple times in the 1600s and is considered one of the first bestsellers in America.

Harriet Powers (1837–1910) was an African American freed slave who created beautiful storytelling quilts in the nineteenth century. She was born into slavery some 30 years before the Civil War. Thanks to a letter written by Harriet that was found in 2009, we know she was a literate woman who turned the well-known stories she read into the stories on her quilts.[10]

FEMINIST FACT

In the early 1800s, the Female Seminary Movement created schools for girls so that they could become good citizens as well as more effective mothers of future citizens and statesmen. Emma Willard (1787–1870) and Catharine E. Beecher (1800–1878) worked to improve the quality of women's education, but this education was open only to those families that could afford it.

Enslaved people in America had no rights at all. Ninety percent lived in the South, where they performed back-breaking work on plantations year-round, up to 18 hours a day. This applied to women, even if they were pregnant, as well as men.[4]

SCIENTISTS

We've looked at women who worked at home, in factories, in fields, and in schools. What about women who worked in labs or at archeological digs or in observatories? Given the lack of science education, it took a combination of talent, grit, and the luck of being born in the right circumstances to the right family to succeed. Let's meet a few female scientists from the seventeenth, eighteenth, and nineteenth centuries.

Maria Cunitz (1610–1664) was born in Silesia, now known as Poland. She became a notable astronomer in addition to raising three sons.

FEMINIST FACT

Many considered Margaret More Roper (1505–1544) the most educated woman of her time in England. Margaret read and translated Greek and Roman texts into English.

SOME FIRSTS IN EDUCATION

In 1837, Oberlin College was the first college to admit women. In 1849, Elizabeth Blackwell (1821–1910) was the first woman to graduate from medical school. In 1866, Lucy Hobbs Taylor (1833–1910) was the first woman to receive a doctor of dental surgery degree, after a long and hard battle. In 1877, Helen Magill White (1853–1944) was the first woman to receive a Ph.D. in America.

She published a book of her work that gained her the reputation of being the most learned woman in astronomy since Hypatia of Alexandria! The Cunitz crater on Venus is named after her.

Émilie du Châtelet (1706–1749) was a brilliant French mathematician, physicist, and author. She wrote a physics textbook and translated some of Isaac Newton's (1643–1727) works, translations that are still relevant today. Unfortunately, like many other women, Émilie died in childbirth at an early age.

Elizabeth Cary Agassiz (1822–1907) was an American naturalist and educator who founded a school for girls in her home. She also helped establish Radcliffe College (now part of Harvard University) for women, who weren't allowed to attend Harvard College.[11]

Madame Curie in her laboratory

Marie Curie (1867–1934) was a French-Polish physicist who discovered radium and did pioneering research into radioactivity. In 1903, she received the Nobel Prize for Physics and, in 1911, she received a second Nobel Prize, this time in chemistry. She was the first woman to win a Nobel Prize, and the first person ever to win twice!

ABOLITION AND THE BEGINNINGS OF CHANGE

As America grew, some women distinguished themselves through their work in the abolitionist movement. As we'll later see, the momentum gained from this movement was the engine behind the first wave of feminism.

The moral outrage of women and men against the enslavement of other humans and their children caught fire in the nineteenth century. Women played a powerful role in abolishing slavery in the United States. Abolitionists, both white and black, fought hard to bring slavery to an end.

Women were a key part of this effort. Quaker women who were encouraged to speak openly about matters of social justice led the revolt. Martha Coffin Wright (1806–1875), Julia Ward Howe (1819–1910), and Mary Livermore (1820–1905) were all on the forefront of the charge against slavery. Many abolitionist women published their writings in the abolitionist newspaper, *The Liberator*.

The role of black abolitionists was equally powerful to that of whites, and much more personal. Runaways as well as freed women joined forces with Philadelphia's Quaker people, who were dedicated to abolishing slavery.

GLOBAL FEMINISM

What about the rest of the world? How are women treated in other countries? What rights and responsibilities do they have? Global feminism, also called world feminism and international feminism, is the worldwide effort on the part of feminists to improve the lives of women everywhere. The issues of global feminism include many of the same rights American women and allies have been striving toward for centuries—gender equality, health care rights, reproductive rights, support for childcare, and a world that is safer and less dangerous for women. In this book, we'll take a look at some of these issues in other countries as we focus on what was happening in the United States.

The first Anti-Slavery Convention of American Women took place in Philadelphia in 1838, at Pennsylvania Hall, only three days after the building's dedication. While women made speeches on this historic day, an angry mob gathered outside and soon began breaking windows with bricks and stones.

The next day, as the numbers and ferocity of the mob grew, women—blacks and whites—linked arms to safely exit the hall and get through the crowd. The mayor of Philadelphia locked the hall's doors and canceled all remaining meetings. Not long after this, the angry mob set fire to the building and burned it to the ground.

Slavery would eventually end, but not before a great deal of bloodshed. The year 1861 was the start of the Civil War, in which Northern states fought to free slaves while Southern Confederate states fought to hold onto the past and its slaves. President Abraham Lincoln (1809–1865) personally supported abolishing slavery.

Pennsylvania Hall was burned to the ground by an angry mob in protest of abolitionism

The Confederacy was destined to fight an uphill battle, as times were changing. The South lost the war and, by the end of 1865, the Thirteenth Amendment to the Constitution was ratified and slavery was abolished.

SENECA FALLS

Until 1848, there had never been a women's rights convention in the United States. The first one took place at the Wesleyan Chapel in Seneca Falls, New York, and boasted 200 women in attendance. Organized by two abolitionists, Lucretia Mott (1793–1880) and Elizabeth Cady Stanton (1815–1902), the Seneca Falls Convention made history.

The call for participants was published in the *Seneca County Courier*.

> "During the first day the meeting will be exclusively for women, who are earnestly invited to attend. The public generally are invited to be present on the second day, when Lucretia Mott, of Philadelphia, and other ladies and gentlemen, will address the Convention."

On July 19, five days after the call went out, hundreds of women gathered in the chapel and listened as Elizabeth Cady Stanton recited the "Declaration of Sentiments and Grievances." Inspired by the Declaration of Independence, this document laid out in detail the injustices against women in this country. Elizabeth wrote it for the convention and used it as a rallying cry to organize women to fight for their rights together.

The convention passed 12 resolutions, 11 unanimously, designed to grant certain rights that women of that time were denied. One resolution—demanding the right to vote—passed narrowly.

The "Declaration of Sentiments" was an important document for the women's movement, but the original papers disappeared after the conference and are still missing. While President Barack Obama was in office, he put out a search called "#FindTheSentiments." You can read about the search at this website.

Obama #findthesentiments

You can read for yourself the "Declaration of Sentiments" at this website. What does it make you think? What is your reaction?

NPS Declaration Sentiments

After the convention, this one resolution demanding the right to vote was ridiculed and resulted in some people withdrawing their support for women's rights. But the convention still marked the beginning of the suffrage movement in America and the first wave of feminism.

At first, newspapers covered the convention with a mocking tone, including this quote from Senator George Graham Vest (1830–1904) of Kentucky: "I want to go home, not to the embrace of some female ward politician, but to the earnest loving look and touch of a true woman." But Elizabeth Cady Stanton correctly predicted that "ridicule would give way to reason."

A statue of the attendees of the Seneca Falls Convention

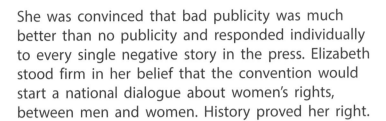

She was convinced that bad publicity was much better than no publicity and responded individually to every single negative story in the press. Elizabeth stood firm in her belief that the convention would start a national dialogue about women's rights, between men and women. History proved her right.

> Swiftly following the convention, regional women's rights meetings sprang up throughout the land.

For example, Lucy Stone (1818–1893), a New England abolitionist, connected the dots between women's rights and anti-slavery activism. To those who criticized her for supposedly taking her energy away from the abolitionist cause by supporting women's rights, she stated, "'I was a woman before I was an abolitionist—I must speak for the women."

The Seneca Falls Convention was a major step on the road to equal rights for women. In the next chapter, we'll see how this energy and enthusiasm resulted in the first wave of feminism, when women demanded the right to vote.

KEY QUESTIONS

- Do you think the reason Sappho's poetry fell out of favor has more to do with her being a woman or a lesbian?
- Why can it be hard to find stories written by women throughout history? What does that say about the relationships between history and power and gender?
- What is the connection between the abolitionist movement and the feminist movement?

INFLUENCE OF SENECA WOMEN

Elizabeth Cady Stanton lived in Seneca Falls, New York, near the Seneca tribal homelands, which was one of the five tribes of the Iroquois Confederation. Through Elizabeth, Native American views toward women greatly influenced what transpired at the Seneca Falls Convention. Native American tribes honor the importance of women, and Iroquois women already possessed many of the rights that the women of Seneca Falls were fighting so hard for. Part of a matriarchal society, Iroquois women had the right to divorce and the right to free speech along with their male counterparts. The idea of equal labor in the "Declaration of Rights and Sentiments" is deeply inspired by Iroquois women who maintained authority in agricultural labor. Historically, it is clear that the goals Elizabeth laid out in the famed "Declaration" is directly influenced by the Iroquois.

Inquire & Investigate

VOCAB LAB

Write down what you think each word means. What root words can you find to help you? What does the context of the word tell you?

abolitionist, benefactor, dialogue, dowry, resolution, and **unanimous**.

Compare your definitions with those of your friends or classmates. Did you all come up with the same meanings? Turn to the text and glossary if you need help.

LETTERS TO THE EDITOR

As Elizabeth Cady Stanton noted, the overwhelmingly negative press in response to the Seneca Falls Convention served as a catalyst for real conversations about women's rights. Around the nation, people were paying attention to women who were calling for an end to inequality. How might Elizabeth's responses to the negative news stories have helped shape the press's continued coverage?

- **With an adult's permission, gather three negative quotes about the convention.** You can find newspaper articles and reactions by going to the library or researching online.

  - What is the general tone of these reactions?

  - Do they tend to come from men or women?

  - Are they respectful, even when negative?

- **Write your own letters to the editor in response to these negative quotes.** How can you expose any prejudice that informed the quotes? Do you choose to use emotion, reason, science, or something else to help prove your points?

> **To investigate more,** find a topic involving women's rights in the news today and compare and contrast the language used now and the language used back then. How are the words, phrases, and tone different? Similar? What about imagery? How are images used to continue the discrimination of women?

Chapter 2 ▶
First-Wave Feminism

How did the right to vote become a turning point in the history of feminism?

WITHOUT THE VOTE, WOMEN'S OPINIONS HELD NO WEIGHT.

IT STARTED STATE BY STATE, BUT WE DIDN'T STOP THERE.

WE WERE AIMING FOR THE NATION.

THEN— THE WORLD!

Without the right to vote, women would have continued to hold far less power than men in the public sphere. The work of suffragists was critical to later stages of the feminist movement.

The Seneca Falls Convention was only the start of the suffrage movement, which ended up being a decades-long struggle. Suffragists wanted women to have the right to vote. Being able to vote is crucial to being a full member of society, with your own representatives holding government offices. What might life be like if women had never gained this right?

At first, suffragists focused only on gaining the right to vote on a state-by-state basis. Eventually, this extended to a national push. Finally, the hard work of the suffragists paid off. On August 26, 1920, the Nineteenth Amendment to the U.S. Constitution was at last ratified.

The amendment declared that women in the United States were entitled to all the rights and responsibilities that come with citizenship, just as their male counterparts. Thanks to the tireless efforts of the suffragists, the women's right to vote became the law of the land.

The battle was not an easy one, but once won, everything else seemed possible. Let's look at how the battle was fought and won by brave women and men.

EARLY ORGANIZING

Two abolitionists stood at the helm of the suffrage movement. Elizabeth Cady Stanton and Susan B. Anthony (1820–1906) were fellow abolitionists who fought for the rights of enslaved people during the period leading up to the Civil War. They also fought passionately to extend voting rights to women, just as they were being extended to black men. But for years, Congress turned a deaf ear.

Elizabeth Cady Stanton and Susan B. Anthony around 1900

> "The World has never yet seen a truly great and virtuous nation because in the degradation of woman the very fountains of life are poisoned at their source."
> —Lucretia Mott

FEMINIST FACT

Some Southern states prevented black women from exercising their right to vote until the 1960s.

After the Civil War, the suffrage movement became more cautious. Some members were afraid of being deemed extremists and shied away from demanding too loudly for the right to vote. They did not want to alienate those in the abolitionist movement who were happy with the victory of "all men" being deemed citizens with unalienable rights.

> It was hard for more moderate women to imagine gaining two victories: one for African Americans and one for women. They believed time, patience, and work within the system were necessary.

In 1869, the suffragist movement split in two. Elizabeth Cady Stanton and Susan B. Anthony created the National Woman Suffrage Association (NWSA). Led by women and based in New York, the NWSA focused its energy and resources on opposing the Fifteenth Amendment, which granted African American men the right to vote but excluded women. The NWSA was considered a radical organization. The American Woman Suffrage Association (AWSA), founded by anti-slavery advocate Lucy Stone and others, took a more moderate approach and included men in its ranks.

Eventually, it became clear that the two opposing suffrage movements were in danger of canceling each other out. In 1890, the organizations merged and became the National American Woman Suffrage Association (NAWSA). Elizabeth was the first to lead this organization. Later, Susan took the helm. Female activists in organizations from the Women's Trade Union League to the Woman's Christian Temperance Union to the National Consumers League supported NAWSA.

TRIAL BY FIRE

In 1869, Susan B. Anthony and Elizabeth Cady Stanton held a singular vision for the NWSA—the passage of an amendment to the U.S. Constitution giving women the right to vote. As the cause dragged on, Susan tried a new method.

On November 5, 1872, she cast a ballot for Ulysses S. Grant (1822–1885) for president of the United States. This took place almost a half century before women were legally granted the right to vote in this country, and she was breaking the law by voting. Susan cast her vote alongside 15 fellow suffragists in Rochester, New York. A few days earlier, she had convinced election officials to register the women.

Elizabeth Cady Stanton, Susan B. Anthony, and Lucretia Mott are carved in marble and displayed at the U.S. Capitol. Artist Adelaide Johnson left the statue unfinished because the fight for women's rights is unfinished as well.

credit: DawesDigital (CC0 BY 1.0)

"There will never be complete equality until women themselves help to make the laws and elect the lawmakers."
—Susan B. Anthony

FEMINIST FACT

In 1872, women could not vote in any state in the Union. Women could, however, vote in the territories of Wyoming (1869) and Utah (1870).

Susan's quiet act of citizenship set off a firestorm trial. The women were arrested after casting their votes. The court put only Susan on trial, rather than all 16 women—she would be tried as an example. Much was riding on this case. If Susan could convince the court that she was entitled to the right to vote, then it could provide a precedent for all women in the United States to vote.

The drama played out before a packed courtroom, during which Susan was charged with violating the Fourteenth Amendment of the Constitution—the amendment that was adopted after the Civil War and which intended to give all citizens, including black Americans, the right to vote.

All male citizens that is.

It forbade any state to deny "the right to vote . . . to any of the male inhabitants" 21 years or older.

> Susan saw a crack in the law. The Fourteenth Amendment also said that, "No state shall make or enforce any law which shall abridge the privileges or immunities of citizens of the United States."

She argued that since women were citizens of the United States, they were entitled to the privilege to vote. Susan's supporters in the courtroom laughed when the district attorney said, after his opening remarks about charging her with voting illegally on November 5, 1872, that, "At that time she was a woman." Susan's lawyer agreed that his client was "indeed a woman."

Despite this brief moment of lightness, the trial bore all the weight of suffrage itself and maintained a serious tone. Susan's lawyer, Henry Selden (1805–1885), argued that his client stood trial for the sole reason of being a woman.

> "If this same act [voting] had been done by her brother, it would have been honorable. But having been done by a woman, it is said to be a crime . . . . I believe this is the first instance in which a woman has been arraigned [accused] in a criminal court merely on account of her sex."

The judge who presided over the case, Ward Hunt (1810–1886), was famous for his opposition to women's suffrage. He refused the defense's request to let Susan take the stand and testify on her own behalf. He ruled that the Fourteenth Amendment allowed only men to vote, and that Susan B. Anthony had voted in violation of the law.

> Instead of allowing the jury to decide whether she was guilty or not, the judge directed the jury to return a guilty verdict, denying Susan a fair trial.

Upon sentencing the next day, the judge allowed Susan to speak. "In your ordered verdict of guilty," she proclaimed, "you have trampled underfoot every vital principle of our government. My natural rights, my civil rights, my political rights, my judicial rights are all alike ignored."

The judge shut her down and angrily ordered her to pay a fine of $100, along with the costs of the prosecution. She answered, "I shall never pay a dollar of your unjust penalty. And I shall earnestly and persistently continue to urge all women . . . that resistance to tyranny is obedience to God."

FEMINIST FACT

Susan B. Anthony did not live to see women gain the vote, but her contributions to the suffrage effort were invaluable. A little more than 100 years later, she was honored by being the face of the newly minted "Susan B. Anthony" silver dollar coin.

Susan stood by her words and refused to pay. Instead of sending her to jail until she obeyed, the judge let her go free. Historians generally agree that had he jailed her, she probably would have appealed the case to a higher court and won on the basis of being denied a fair trial by jury. The judge cleverly denied her this option, and that was the end of Susan B. Anthony's case.

THE WEST IS WON

After Susan's trial and the merging of the NWSA and the AWSA into the NAWSA, the suffragists once again took a state-by-state approach to gain the vote for women. By 1910, only the West was won, with five states—Wyoming, Utah, Colorado, Idaho, and Washington—approving suffrage.

Susan B. Anthony on her front porch in Adams, Massachusetts, surrounded by other early feminists, 1896

Some historians believe that the small populations of these states made them easier to organize. The frontier needed more women, and states that supported suffrage could probably attract more of them. As more years passed, two future congresswomen—Ruth Hanna McCormick (1888–1944) of Illinois and Jeannette Rankin (1880–1973) of Montana—helped gain the vote for women in their states.

> Old-fashioned legwork
> led to Jeannette Rankin becoming
> the first female member of Congress.
> She traveled by train and stopped at
> one-room schoolhouses, potluck
> suppers, local ranches, and
> anywhere else she could to reach
> Montana's scattered population.

Her brother was a prominent politician, so his influence certainly helped. However, it was her own persistence that landed her the job in 1916.

When Alice Paul stepped down as head of the congressional committee for the NAWSA, Ruth Hanna McCormick stepped up and served as leader from 1913 to 1914. She stayed involved in politics, and from 1919 to 1924 served as the chairman of the first woman's executive committee of the Republican National Committee and an associate member of the national committee. Ruth was elected as a Republican to the 71st Congress, representing Illinois, from 1929 to 1931.

FREDERICK DOUGLASS

Frederick Douglass (c.1818–1895) is considered by many to be an American hero who fought many battles, including his steadfast dedication to the fight for women's rights. He escaped slavery in Maryland in 1838 and went on to become a leader in the abolitionist movement. During the first woman's rights convention in Seneca Falls in 1848, Frederick was one of the few men present. He remained a lifelong ally of Elizabeth Cady Stanton and Susan B. Anthony.

In April 1888, Frederick gave a speech before the International Council of Women in Washington, DC.

"It may be kind to tell them that our cause has passed beyond the period of arguing. The demand of the hour is not argument, but assertion, firm and inflexible assertion, assertion which has more than the force of an argument."[2]

VOTING IN EUROPE

Women in several European countries were granted the right to vote in the early years of the twentieth century, for example, Finland (1906), Denmark and Iceland (1915), and Austria, Czechoslovakia, Poland, Sweden and Britain (1918). In Britain, women had to be older than 30 until this was changed to 21 in 1928 (in contrast to men, who just had to be 21 in 1918). Other European countries did not give women the vote until much later: France in 1944, Switzerland in 1971, and Liechtenstein in 1984. Countries in other parts of the world were also slow to allow women to vote, for example, Japan (1945), Argentina (1946), and China (1947). In Saudi Arabia—which rarely has elections—women were not allowed to vote or run for office until King Abdullah (1924–2015) granted them the right in 2011.[1]

Alice Paul, 1915

MORE FACTIONS ARISE

Many activists found their patience tested by the slow pace of progress, and some of them took stronger action. In 1913, Alice Paul, described in the introduction to this book, formed the Congressional Union for Woman Suffrage, whose name was later changed to the National Women's Party.

The party began to put pressure on the government for a federal equal rights amendment. The members of this organization had decided that the state-by-state approach wasn't progressing fast enough.

In contrast, the NAWSA aligned itself with President Woodrow Wilson (1856–1924) and his war effort. President Wilson was trying to garner public support for entering the Great War, later called World War I, that was raging in Europe. Many notable suffragists, including Jeannette Rankin of Montana, were pacifists. They didn't believe war was the answer to society's problems. However, they decided that strategically it was better to support President Wilson than to go against him.

America's involvement in World War I slowed the suffragists' campaign, but also helped them advance their cause.

The governor of Colorado ratifies the Nineteenth Amendment as women look on.

Some activists argued that women's work on behalf of the war effort proved that they were just as patriotic and deserving of citizenship as men. Women were working in munitions factories, in hospitals, in clerical positions—taking on the jobs and responsibilities left behind by the men who had gone to fight.

Activists also believed that if President Wilson chose not to come through for them, they could pull out of the war effort just when they were needed most.

Women had to wait until the spring of 1919, after the war ended in November 1918, for a voting rights amendment to pass Congress. A year later, on August 26, 1920, the Nineteenth Amendment was ratified when Tennessee became the 36th state to approve it. This amendment provided full voting rights for women in the entire country.

THE RIGHT TO VOTE, AT LONG LAST!

When the Nineteenth Amendment was ratified in 1920, granting all American women the right to vote, it represented a hard-won battle. Decades and decades of writing, lecturing, lobbying, marching, and protesting finally led to this necessary change to the Constitution. Few early pioneers in the women's movement lived to see this victory.

You might think the right to vote would be the beginning of radical changes in women's lives. But, just as change can be hard-fought, the tides of history can erect unforeseen barriers.

When Tennessee became the 36th state to ratify the Nineteenth Amendment on August 18, 1920, Alice Paul unfurled the ratification banner from suffrage headquarters.

Before the next tidal wave of feminism would begin in the middle of the twentieth century, much would occur. Women would take two steps forward, one step back in the march toward equal rights.

KEY QUESTIONS

- Are you surprised that men joined the suffrage movement? What are some ways men support women today?

- Why was it more dangerous to be a black suffragist than a white suffragist? What point was Sojourner Truth making when she asked, "Ain't I a woman?"

WRITE YOUR POLITICIAN

Suffragists did a lot of letter writing as they fought for women's right to vote. This was before email and social media, so their letters were written on paper and sent by mail. In today's world, politicians receive lots of communications about different causes that people feel strongly about. Add your voice!

- **Choose a topic that you feel strongly about.** This can be climate change, immigration, war, human rights, or something else.

- **At the library or on the internet, do some research on your chosen topic.** Who are the major players with the power to effect change? What are their views on the topic? Do different people have different viewpoints?

- **Choose one person who agrees with your views and another person who has the opposite views.** Write each of them a letter explaining your position. What can you write to get them to agree with you? How can you show your support for the person whose values align with yours?

- **Read the letters aloud to a friend or classmate.** See if they can guess who it is you're writing to. Do they think your letters were convincing?

> **To investigate more,** imagine how one or more of the historical figures from this chapter would collaborate with a feminist, real or imagined, of today? What would feminists past and present focus on together in the twenty-first century?

Chapter 3

Between the Waves

ONCE WE GOT THE VOTE, SO MANY DOORS WERE OPENED.

What was the next step for the women's movement after gaining the right to vote?

BUT THE COURSE OF HISTORY WOULD AFFECT EVERYTHING.

THE BOOM OF THE '20s...

THE GREAT DEPRESSION....

AND ESPECIALLY OUR ROLE IN WORLD WAR II HAD A BIG IMPACT ON THE COURSE OF OUR RIGHTS!

Women still had work to do to gain an equal standing in society, but this work was interrupted by the Great Depression and World War II. During these decades, women's fight for equality was overshadowed by a national struggle to survive.

The hard-won victory for women's suffrage marked the peak of the first wave of feminism in the United States, but the second wave did not occur until the 1960s and 1970s. What happened in between? Were women happy with their roles and content enough to give up the fight?

Well, that wasn't quite the case. But an economic collapse that began in 1929 and lasted a decade, followed by World War II, distracted American citizens and people around the world from issues of feminism. Instead of marching, protesting, hosting conferences, and working to get women into positions of political power, women were trying to help feed their families.

THE ROARING TWENTIES

The Nineteenth Amendment was ratified in 1920, just as the Jazz Age was being ushered in. World War I was over and people wanted to enjoy their lives and spend their money.

The 1920s were a period of "anything goes" for the youth of America. As the country prospered in the early years of the twentieth century, a youth culture arose to an embrace of carefree enjoyment and a more liberal outlook on life.

The year 1920 was marked not only by women's right to vote, but also by the beginning of Prohibition. The Eighteenth Amendment to the constitution banned the distribution of many types of alcohol.

You might think this meant people's social lives suffered and the nation grew quiet and sober, but the opposite happened.

New York City Deputy Police Commissioner John A. Leach, right, watching agents pour liquor into a sewer following a raid during the height of Prohibition

credit: retrieved from Library of Congress

Because alcohol was no longer legal, bootlegging—the illegal production and sale of alcohol—became common. Underground establishments called speakeasies rose up, and the decade of the 1920s became associated with drinking, rollicking jazz music, and a newfound free-spiritedness. And women? What were they doing?

As during other decades, no single definition captures what it meant to be a woman in the United States during the 1920s. While the passage of the Nineteenth Amendment opened the door to greater participation in government and a louder voice for women in general, different types of women emerged as unique voices during this time of transition.

> The "new woman" embraced the "new morality," which placed great value on personal freedom.

"Flappers" were the young, fashion-forward women who cut their hair in bobs and changed women's clothing styles for years to come. Clara Bow (1905–1965), a silent movie actress, who was given the nickname the "It Girl," embodied the look and free spirit of the times.

The new woman not only exercised her right to vote—she also went to college and joined the workforce. Women of the 1920s took jobs as factory workers, secretaries, sales clerks, and telephone operators. The number of women attending college rose throughout the decade.

Some women were traditionalists who preferred to stick to old-fashioned family values—these women believed that a woman's place was still in the home.

Clara Bow, 1924

credit: retrieved from Library of Congress

They feared that the changes in women's roles would lead to the destruction of conservative and religious moral values. Other women held a whole range of values between these two extremes.

Black American women's lives were transformed during this era as well, as more black women made the move from rural to urban areas.

The Harlem Renaissance, which was an explosion of new and exciting music, literature, and art by black artists, didn't just affect those in New York City, but spread across the country. It became an iconic movement in which many female jazz singers, most of them black, gained fame while creating some of the most important music of the twentieth century.

During the Jazz Age, Josephine Baker dances the Charleston in 1926.

credit: French Walery

The song "Brother, Can You Spare a Dime?" became the theme song of the 1930s. Listen to a version at this website. What do the lyrics tell you about the values and priorities of the era? What would the theme song of the current era be?

 NPR Depression era anthem

THE COLLAPSE

The Jazz Age abruptly ended and everything changed on October 29, 1929. Black Friday was the day of the greatest stock market crash in history. On this day, after years of excess, the stock market plunged to its lowest point in American history. Overnight, the country went from being a land of plenty to a land of poverty.

Desperate bankers and investors, hopeless and penniless, jumped from skyscrapers to their deaths. The country entered the Great Depression, a period of time that lasted for the next 10 years.

The high-minded ideals of the first-wave feminists were set on the back burner as families struggled to put food on the table. Men, the traditional breadwinners, lost their jobs and were forced to seek charity or take whatever menial labor they could find just to pay the rent or buy bread.

As if economic devastation weren't enough, parts of the country suffered environmental devastation as well. When the Great Depression began at the end of the 1920s, the prices for wheat plunged. Desperate farmers in the Midwest dug up more and more grassland to plant more wheat in a pointless attempt to break even. When a terrible drought hit in 1931, the soil began to blow away. This led to terrifying dust storms. What became known as the "Dust Bowl" covered large areas of Colorado, Kansas, Texas, Oklahoma, and New Mexico.

During the Great Depression of the 1930s, women sought out and took whatever jobs they could to help keep their families afloat. Women faced the prejudice of employers who were nervous about hiring women for jobs that had been traditionally held by men. Some women were even blamed for taking away jobs from men.

FEMINIST FACT

"It looked like twisters, just rows of twisters. I thought whatever it is, this is the end. You couldn't see anything except when you brushed someone's hair. There were sparks because of the electricity in the air. That's how you identified where anybody was."

—Rosa Becker, recalling her experience as a teenager during the Dust Bowl[3]

A farm buried in dust in South Dakota, 1936

credit: U.S. Department of Agriculture

The War Manpower Commission formed a women's advisory committee to strategize the best ways to use female labor to help in the war. The committee aimed to target married women who lived in metropolitan areas, even those who'd never worked outside the home before. The idea was to remove the stigma attached to the idea of women working.

credit: Ann Rosener, U.S. Office of War Information

Depression-era women, if they could, were likely to seek out higher education to gain the skills they needed to better support themselves and their families. Without these skills, they were given jobs considered to be more typically female, such as cooking, cleaning, and childcare.

As farmers lost their crops and livelihood in the Dust Bowl of the 1930s and city folk went bankrupt, the country's population had little to hope for. Only survival mattered. Social progress for women hit a standstill as putting food on the table became America's number one priority. Feminism would have to wait.

GOING TO WAR

When the United States joined the Allies in World War II in 1941, all attention turned to the war effort. Because of the war, the country experienced an economic boom—and not just for men. Women benefitted, too. President Franklin Roosevelt (1882–1945) ordered the formation of the War Manpower Commission (WMC) in 1942 to organize workers to meet the needs of the country both at war and at home.

In greater numbers than ever, women went to work in jobs that had been traditionally held by men. Many went to work in defense plants and in the aircraft industry. Many more went to work in offices and factories, replacing men who had been sent to the front lines.

Still more women were needed to do crucial jobs, so the U.S. government created a promotional figure called Rosie the Riveter, a figure who was both pretty and tough. Rosie was part of a campaign to recruit female workers to the munitions factories. The government also sponsored childcare facilities so parents could feel secure leaving their children to go to work.

Overseas in England, women were performing a unique job helping win the war. The Allies faced a difficult problem during World War II—they were unable to decode the messages Nazi Germany was sending about its military plans and movement. It was information the Allies really needed to help their cause.

To solve this problem, a top-secret project took place at Bletchley Park in England.

While many male scientists, cryptanalysts, and mathematicians—including Alan Turing (1912–1954), a famous mathematician and computer scientist—worked at Bletchley, about 8,000 women were also involved. The women played key roles in operating communications equipment, intercepting and translating messages, and performing many other critical tasks.

Some women were highly educated, with degrees in mathematics and physics. One woman, Joan Clarke (1917–1996), was given several awards for her contribution to the Enigma project that finally decrypted Germany's secret communications. Not until the 1970s could those who worked at Bletchley talk about their work there![4]

FEMINIST FACT

More than 1,000 women served as Women's Airforce Service Pilots (WASPs) during World War II and 38 lost their lives. As the first women to fly military aircraft, they transported planes the long distances from factories to military bases. Not until 1977, however, were the WASPs granted military status! In 2010 they received Congressional Gold Medals.[5]

POST-WAR LIVING

Once World War II ended in 1945, the United States went through a cultural shift. The men came home from war. Many of them entered college as a result of the G.I. Bill, or the Serviceman's Readjustment Act of 1944, which funded college educations for returning veterans. With or without college degrees, men were able to get jobs that paid decent wages. A time of peace and prosperity began.

As the men came back from serving in the war, all of the jobs that women had been doing for the past four years went to these men. Women were expected to give up their spots in the factories, offices, and plants. A similar situation had occurred after World War I.

In the 1940s and 1950s, the economy was still booming, so there were still jobs that needed to be filled even after the men came home. Those women who wanted to could usually find work. However, many of them chose to follow a more traditional route and stay home.

> As families felt more secure, they had more children and the baby boom began. Many women became housewives and mothers as men went off to work.

Remember Margaret Fuller's idealistic dreams, mentioned in Chapter 2, of an independent woman in union with an independent man? For much of American society in the 1940s and 1950s, these ideals now seemed dated and impractical. In most families, men made the money while women took care of the children and the home.

INTERESTING JOBS

During World War II, the Nazis were constantly trying to hunt down spies—especially American Virginia Hall (1906–1982). Called the "limping lady" due to her wooden prosthetic leg, Virginia worked as a spy for the British in German-occupied France. She had lived in France and was fluent in French and German. Pretending to be a journalist, Virginia was exceptionally skilled at obtaining information about German troop movements. Although the Nazi hunt forced her to flee France, she returned as part of the OSS (now the CIA). Disguised as an old woman, she organized sabotage missions such as blowing up bridges. For her service, Virginia received the Distinguished Service Cross—the only woman to do so during World War II.[6]

Suburbs sprang up outside major cities and the American Dream flourished. For many people, that dream was a house filled with modern appliances, a husband whose main responsibility was earning money and serving as head of the household, and a wife and mother who took care of the home and children.

BUY THIS!

As suburbia spread in the 1950s, so did the popularity of television and with it, advertising. This highly lucrative business made most of its money selling products in the new leisure economy. Families had the money to buy products and services they'd never considered before.

> Television advertising became a new canvas on which the unequal roles of men and women were displayed.

Ads for cars and cigarettes were aimed at men, while ads for home appliances, cleaning products, and food were aimed at female consumers. Even though women did not have the economic power they have today—women could not get a credit card in their own name until 1974—they did have influence over their husbands. They could talk their husbands into spending money on the products they saw advertised on television.

THE FEMININE MYSTIQUE

How did this world of suburban housewives lead to the second wave of feminism? Most people believe it began with a book.

FEMINIST FACT

You might think that times have changed, but as recently as 2017, Audi, the German car manufacturer, released a commercial in China that compared buying a car to choosing a wife. Some people believed the message behind this commercial was that women are still seen as property.

VOCAB LAB

Write down what you think each word means. What root words can you find to help you? What does the context of the word tell you?

drought, **flapper**, **Great Depression**, **iconic**, **menial labor**, **prejudice**, **speakeasy**, and **stigma**.

Compare your definitions with those of your friends or classmates. Did you all come up with the same meanings? Turn to the text and glossary if you need help.

Betty Friedan (1921–2006) was an American wife, mother, writer, and activist living during the time of the economic boom after World War II. Born in Peoria, Illinois, mere months after the passage of the 1920 amendment that gave women the right to vote, she is best known for her 1963 book, *The Feminine Mystique*. The book shared many stories of women who felt sad and guilty even as their families flourished.

Betty herself shared those feelings. A graduate of Smith College, Betty had worked as a journalist, but left the field to spend time at home raising two sons while her husband went to work. At home, she began to experience a problem she could not put words to.

Soon, she found that other housewives confided in her. These women supposedly had it all—a husband, children, financial security, health, and wealth. What more could they want?

And yet, Betty heard stories such as the following.

> "Each suburban wife struggled with it alone as she made the beds, shopped for groceries, matched slipcover material, ate peanut butter sandwiches with her children, chauffeured Cub Scouts and Brownies, lay beside her husband at night. She was afraid to even ask of herself the silent question: 'Is this all?'"

Betty observed, "Some said it was the old problem—education. More and more women had education, which naturally made them unhappy in their role as housewives." She noted that a male humorist joked in the July 1960 issue of *Harper's Bazaar* that this undefinable problem women were having could be remedied by taking away the vote.

The Feminine Mystique made many women realize they weren't alone in feeling unhappy in their suburban lives. They formed what were called consciousness-raising groups, where they shared stories of isolation and depression with other women. They began to discuss the cause of their problems and ways they could find greater happiness in their lives and in their marriages.

> They began to look inward and recognize that they wanted more out of their lives.

As the post-war years went by, women began to recognize the need for a new push toward equality for the sexes. Now they had the right to vote, they looked at other ways they could improve the lives of individuals and groups, including ways to improve marriages and family life, further their professional lives, and gain and exercise reproductive rights.

KEY QUESTIONS

- Why was feminism out of the spotlight for a few decades? What might have happened had women maintained the push for equal rights during this time?

- What kind of influence did advertising have on people during the 1950s? Do you think there's more or less influence through advertising today? Why or why not?

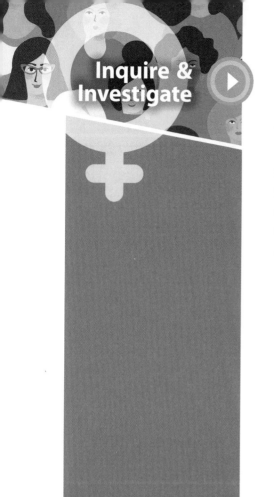

IN CONTEXT

No social movement occurs in a vacuum. Historical events such as wars impact whether a movement succeeds or slows. How did the Great Depression affect the women's movement? How did World War II affect it?

- **Do some research on the Great Depression.** Take notes as you search the internet and read material from the library.

  - How did women's lives change during the 1930s?

  - How did men's lives change?

  - Did women move from place to place?

  - What kinds of jobs were available for women?

  - How did having children impact a woman's ability to support herself and her family?

  - What do you think was the main concern for women during this period?

- **Do some research on how World War II changed the lives of women.** Consider the following questions.

  - What happened when World War II began? How did women's lives change?

  - How did families change as a result of the war?

  - What kinds of jobs were available to women that hadn't been previously?

  - What happened after the war ended?

- **After doing your research, consider if these historical events hadn't happened.** Write up a paragraph on what women's roles might have looked like without these influences.

> **To investigate more,** search for film clips from the Great Depression. How did this decade differ visually from today? What particular challenges did women face as opposed to men? How can you tell from the film?

Chapter 4
The Second Wave

FIRST WAVE, VOTES, SECOND WAVE, SELVES!

How did the second wave of feminism differ from the first?

WITH THE VOTE, WE COULD VOICE OUR POLITICAL OPINIONS.

BUT WHAT ABOUT OUR OWN RIGHTS?

THERE WERE STILL A LOT OF LIMITS ON US.

THE NEXT WAVE OF FEMINISM WAS FOCUSED ON EXACTLY THAT!

While the first wave of feminism focused mainly on the right to vote, the second wave aimed to improve the lives of women in different, often more personal ways.

As we learned in Chapter 2, the first wave of feminism emerged from the abolitionist movement. Similarly, the seeds of the second wave of feminism were planted during the civil rights and anti-Vietnam War movements. As people took to the streets to fight against injustice, the energy to fight for women's rights was renewed.

This time, however, women were fighting for something different from the right to vote. They wanted choices—when to have children, what jobs to perform, where to go to school, how their marriages and other relationships worked, and how society viewed them. They also wanted greater representation in politics.

THE NOW BILL OF RIGHTS

Betty Friedan's book sparked the second wave of feminism. She would become a key figure as the women's movement grew in momentum.

Women marching in 1970

credit: Warren K. Leffler *U.S. News & World Report*

In 1966, she cofounded NOW, the National Organization for Women. The feminist group still holds political influence more than 50 years after its founding.

In 1968, NOW issued a bill of rights. Its mission was to present the bill of rights to all political candidates running for office. The members of NOW would judge these candidates by their support of NOW's agenda for women's rights.

The main issues on NOW's agenda included the following.

- The passage of the Equal Rights Amendment, which would help enforce the prohibitions against sex discrimination in employment.

- Maternity leave rights and other forms of support for working parents, such as daycare centers.

- Job training for women in poverty.

- The right of women to control their reproductive lives.

Feminists demonstrating for their rights became associated with burning bras in protest of items that symbolized women's oppression. But did they really burn their bras? Read this article to find out. What do you think of this type of protest?

🔍 BBC bra burning

These issues would become the key focus of second-wave feminism. However, as the women's liberation, or "women's lib," movement grew, more and more women began to criticize Betty Friedan for being a privileged, white, suburban housewife. For the movement to become stronger, these women believed that it needed to expand and become more inclusive of people from diverse ethnicities, backgrounds, and classes.

Many women of color were drawn to the women's movement because of economic issues. As disenfranchised minorities, they understood all too well that it was usually women who were expected to care for children, along with earning the money to feed them. Many women of color had been involved in the civil rights movement, and were already in a frame of mind to fight for women's rights.

But soon, the relationship between women of color and the larger women's movement began to splinter.

Women of color began to form their own groups where they could focus on issues that affected them more than the population of women as a whole. Activist Linda Burnham (1948–) recalls,

"We started Black Sisters United, and it was basically a consciousness-raising group. We were struggling to understand what was different about our perspective on women's place in the world from what we were hearing from the mainstream women's movement. And we couldn't have that conversation in spaces that were majority white women."

Racism topped the list of issues that white women, because of the color of their skin, could ignore, but which women of color could not. Women of color appreciated meeting with each other and talking openly about the ways in which the mainstream feminist movement was not serving them. For instance, privileged, white women often spoke about child-rearing as an obligation and burden they were saddled with, whereas many black women saw the family as a refuge.

Similarly, because of the United States' history of eugenics and forced sterilization of black women, birth control was looked upon as something to be explored with skepticism. While many white women saw only freedom in a pill that could prevent pregnancy, many black women felt more cautious.

THE ERA: HOPE AND FAILURE

We learned in Chapter 2 about how the Equal Rights Amendment was first proposed by Alice Paul of the National Women's Party in 1923. In 1970, NOW made the ratification of the amendment a top priority. Feminists of this period saw ratification as the only real way to eliminate all legal, gender-based discrimination in the United States.

> Laws that made it possible for employers to treat women differently from men had to go.

The U.S. House of Representatives approved the measure in 1970, and the U.S. Senate did the same two years later. It looked as though victory was inevitable. By 1973, 30 states of the required 38 had voted in favor of ratifying the amendment.

CONSCIOUSNESS-RAISING

Consciousness-raising (C-R) is a tool that some members of the women's liberation movement adopted from the civil rights movement in the 1960s, where it was also called "telling it like it is." In C-R, women answer a question using examples from their personal lives and then the group uses these personal testimonies to draw conclusions about the political root of women's so-called "personal" problems.

> **"Feminism is doomed to failure because it is based on an attempt to repeal and restructure human nature."**
> **—Phyllis Schlafly**

And then came the STOP ERA campaign. Phyllis Schlafly (1924–2016), a white woman who was educated as a lawyer, led the movement as she crusaded for traditional values and painted the ERA as a threat to these values.

Phyllis was media-savvy and talented at public speaking. She often opened her speeches with barbed jokes such as, "I'd like to thank my husband for letting me be here tonight."

Phyllis used scare tactics, claiming that laws that protect women would be abolished if the ERA was ratified. Under the ERA, she argued, women could be drafted into fighting a war along with men. Women might lose alimony and the likelihood of gaining child custody in divorce cases, she claimed.

Phyllis Schlafly, 1977

credit: Warren K. Leffler *U.S. News & World Report*

Her methods worked. By 1982, the year the amendment expired, only 35 states had voted in favor of the ERA. Feminists lost by three states. The failure of the ERA to pass was a huge blow to the feminist movement.

IN THE WORKPLACE

One challenge that women faced in daily life was the difficulty in gaining financial independence. This was hard for several reasons. Women were at the receiving end of discriminatory practices, such as not being hired if they were pregnant. There was also still somewhat of a stigma to women working outside the home.

Women simply weren't paid as much as men for doing the same jobs. Plus, the professions that were welcoming to females, such as teacher, daycare provider, and nurse, were the professions that made less money than those traditionally associated with men—lawyers, doctors, and company presidents.

> One thing that helped level the playing field and make it fairer for women in the workplace was the passage of the Equal Pay Act in 1963, which made it illegal for employers to pay women less than men for the same job.

Then, just a year later, the government passed Title VII of the Civil Rights Act of 1964, which made it illegal to discriminate in the workplace on the basis of race and gender. Even as the general attitude was slow to change, at least women had the law on their side when it came to getting the same jobs and being paid the same wages as men.

BIRTH CONTROL AND ABORTIONS

Sexuality and reproduction were another major component of second-wave feminism. For women, sex was a risk—they could get pregnant, which could derail their goals of going to school, working, or choosing when to have a family. Abortion, which is a way of ending a pregnancy before birth, was illegal. If a woman got pregnant, her only options were to have the baby (and possibly give it up for adoption) or seek an illegal procedure, which could be dangerous and even deadly.

A first-wave feminist named Margaret Sanger (1879–1966) was one of the key people who worked to change that. A nurse and educator, she opened the first birth control clinic in the United States in 1916. The clinic later evolved into the Planned Parenthood Federation of America.

> American culture and the Catholic Church, both of which held quite a lot of political power, were morally opposed to birth control, but during the second wave of feminism the tide began to turn.

In the 1950s, scientist Gregory Pincus (1903–1967) and fertility doctor John Rock (1890–1984) created what is now known as the pill—the oral contraceptive that will forever be associated with the sexual revolution. Gregory had met Margaret Sanger in 1950 and it was she who urged him to work on the pill's development. She even helped him raise $150,000 for research.[1] In 1960, the U.S. Food and Drug Administration approved this first oral contraceptive.

The pill could be taken daily by women to prevent them from getting pregnant. The new drug at last allowed women to exert some control over their bodies and decide when or if to have a child.

While FDA approval was a huge step, problems still existed. The pill wasn't widely available, and in 1965, the U.S. Supreme Court ruled that only married women had the right to use birth control. What about all of the unmarried women?

> Feminists were on the front lines of the effort to improve access to the pill. Finally, in 1972, the Supreme Court approved the use of birth control for all women, married or not.

Abortion was another significant aspect of second-wave feminism. During the turbulent 1960s, the United States had no standard abortion regulations. Some states allowed it, while others outlawed it. Feminists rallied to make abortion legal to avoid the medical repercussions, including death, that could happen when women sought out illegal abortions.

In 1973, the Supreme Court heard the case of the anonymous Jane Roe. She was an unmarried Texas mother who claimed the state violated her privacy rights guaranteed by the Fourteenth Amendment by banning the practice of abortion.

Roe v. Wade was a landmark Supreme Court decision that established a woman's legal right to an abortion, often called the legal right to choose. The court ruled in Roe's favor in a 7–2 decision. *Roe v. Wade* became the law of the land, but to this day, both the law and the procedure still provoke heated debate and controversy.

LEGAL ABORTIONS

For America's first 100 years, abortion was not a subject of debate. In the seventeenth and eighteenth centuries, it was not uncommon for women to take drugs known as "female monthly pills" if they wanted to end their pregnancies. However, these drugs were only occasionally effective and sometimes even fatal. Abortions became illegal nationwide between 1860 and 1880, when the American Medical Association deemed abortions unsafe and immoral unless the woman was under the care of a doctor. Many scholars believe that doctors simply wanted to eliminate competition. By the 1930s, states were strictly enforcing anti-abortion laws.

RADICAL FEMINISM

The W.I.T.C.H. (Women's International Conspiracy from Hell) movement was founded on Halloween in 1968. Members dressed as witches for their first event in 1969 to protest capitalism and place a hex on the financial district on Wall Street. Although they believed in many causes, from civil rights to students' rights, women's rights were a top priority. A few months after the Wall Street action, they released white mice at Madison Square Garden to protest a bridal fair they believe kept women trapped in traditional roles. The group, whose members were anonymous, disbanded in 1970 but then came back together in 2016 in response to the presidency of Donald Trump.

Just as the first-wave feminists didn't always agree with each other on the best way of doing things, the second-wave feminists had disagreements as well. One way in which feminists didn't see eye to eye was in the level of societal disruption needed to make change.

Feminists such as Betty Friedan were focused on working with politicians and other leaders to change laws or make new laws that better supported women in all areas of life, such as how much money they earned compared to men. Other feminists, such as Kate Millet (1934–2017), believed that working from within existing legal and societal structures didn't accomplish anything. These feminists became known as radical feminists, and they focused on the goal of dismantling the patriarchy.

The patriarchy is the concept that society is ruled by men and men's needs. A family patriarch is the father, husband, or other male figure who guides the family. For society, that male figure could be the president or other politicians, the male heads of business, or any other male figure who holds a leadership role. A patriarchal society is one in which much of the power is held by men.

That's why, radical feminists argued, change couldn't happen within current systems—these were all built on the idea that men were innately more powerful than women. These feminists believed the structures themselves had to be torn down before real equality could be achieved.

Radical feminists believed that women were part of the problem. Kate Millet argues, as Margaret Fuller had before her, that for too long, women had accepted the roles assigned to them instead of going against societal norms and challenging the idea that men should automatically be in charge.

MEET THE PIONEERS

Throughout the second wave, individual women served as trailblazers and role models to show women and girls how to keep taking steps forward. Let's look at a few key figures.

Author and activist Rita Mae Brown (1944–) knew firsthand how it felt to be excluded from a cause she cared about. Born into poverty, Rita went to college on scholarship and was expelled from the racially segregated University of Florida at Gainesville in 1964 for participating in a civil rights protest. After finding her way to New York City, she excelled at New York University and became involved in the student Homophile League at Columbia.

> She eventually left because she was treated differently because she was a lesbian.

Rita went on to become a dedicated leader of the feminist cause and for the fight for gay and lesbian rights. She was an integral part of the lavender menace protest in 1970.

Like Betty Friedan, Gloria Steinem (1934–) graduated from Smith College and worked as a journalist. In 1971, she and Betty, along with Shirley Chisholm (1924–2005), Bella Abzug (1920–1988), and others, formed the National Women's Political Caucus.

THE LAVENDER MENACE

During the second wave, many lesbians, bisexuals, transgender, and nonbinary people felt unwelcome by the mainstream feminists. They felt that their needs and ideas were being ignored. They weren't wrong—Betty Friedan, who believed that mainstream approval was critical to success, famously called lesbian feminists the "lavender menace." Some lesbians held a funny protest in response to remarks made by Betty Friedan and the exclusive policies of NOW. The Second Congress to Unite Women event took place on May 1, 1970. Lesbians were not invited. But many showed up secretly. At a precise moment, the lights were turned off. When they were turned back on, 17 lesbians wearing "Lavender Menace" T-shirts were standing in the aisles. Most of the audience responded with laughter and calls to join.

The National Women's
Political Caucus was dedicated to
the cause of women's issues.

GOLDA MEIR

Golda Meir (1898–1978) was a key role model to women and girls during the second wave of feminism. She was born in Ukraine, moved to Wisconsin when young, and then emigrated to Palestine in 1921. She was always politically active and was involved in the Zionist movement that led to the foundation of the State of Israel in 1948. After serving as minister of labor and foreign minister, she was prime minister of Israel from 1969 to 1974. She worked hard for peace in the Middle East by diplomatic means, but was unsuccessful.[6] Do you think many women led countries then?

Listen to Golda Meir speaking about the problems in the Middle East.

 YouTube Meir becomes PM

In 1969, Gloria Steinem wrote an essay for *New York Magazine* called "After Black Power, Women's Liberation," which many feminists considered a call to arms. Gloria's glamorous appearance made her a natural leader for a movement looking for a face, though her glamour also worked against her. She was not always considered serious or political enough for the second-wave movement she helped launch.

Gloria is best known for her role in launching *Ms.* magazine in 1972, which took on women's issues in a direct way, as no American magazine had before. *Ms.* taught integrity by example—the editorial board refused to run advertisements. Remember what you learned about the ways advertisers marketed differently to men and women? That wasn't going to happen in this magazine!

In November 1968, NOW member Shirley Chisholm became the first black woman elected to the U.S. House of Representatives. An early member of NOW, Shirley dedicated her energy to enlarging the federal government's food stamp program for low-income families. She pioneered the Special Supplemental Nutrition Program for Women, Infants and Children (WIC). This program is still thriving today and provides support for pregnant women, filling a gap left by other programs.

All staff Shirley hired for her office were women and half of them were black. Shirley said that she had faced much more discrimination during her New York legislative career because she was a woman than because of her race.[7]

Poets and authors made a big splash during the second wave and pushed ideas forward through art. Audre Lorde (1934–1992) was a black lesbian, poet, social justice activist, and radical feminist.

> In her poetry and nonfiction writing, Audre calls attention to the idea that thinking about men and women as being completely separate and opposite is a limiting way of looking at gender. She also questions the simplistic idea of a unified women's movement.

In her poem "Afterimages," Audre writes the following stanza, in which she feels connection with other women who have suffered.

> Within my eyes
>
> the flickering afterimages of a nightmare rain
>
> a woman wrings her hands
>
> beneath the weight of agonies remembered
>
> I wade through summer ghosts
>
> betrayed by vision
>
> hers and my own
>
> becoming dragonfish to survive
>
> the horrors we are living
>
> with tortured lungs

Radical feminist poet and essayist Adrienne Rich (1929–2012) was born to a white, middle-class family. Following her doctor father's and concert pianist mother's ambitions for her, she studied at Radcliffe, married a Harvard professor, and had three children.

MUSIC

You've probably heard of the Beatles and Rolling Stones, bands that changed the course of music significantly in the 1960s and 1970s. Many female artists were extremely popular and successful, too. Some, such as Joan Baez (1941–), were civil rights and anti-war activists. Many of the most successful singers were African American women such as Nina Simone (1933–2003), Diana Ross (1944–), Gladys Knight (1944–), and the legendary Aretha Franklin (1942–2018).

Listen to Simone singing "Young, Gifted, and Black."

Simone young gifted

And listen to Aretha Franklin singing at President Obama's 2009 inauguration.

Franklin Obama inauguration

Adrienne wrote and published poetry from a young age, but it followed a more classic style. Her marriage grew troubled in the 1960s, when she became aware of the political climate all around her. Her poetry became more radicalized then as well.

Adrienne's husband died in 1970, and, six years later, she began living with her long-term partner, Michelle Cliff (1946–2016). The year 1976 also marked the publication of Adrienne's book of essays, *Of Woman Born: Motherhood as Institution and Experience*, which influenced a generation of feminists.

> As the 1970s wound down and a new decade began, how did feminism fare? Did the different factions find ways of working together toward common goals? Did women finally achieve true equality in America?

We'll look at the period of backlash that followed the second wave of feminism in the next chapter.

KEY QUESTIONS

- Why did Phyllis Schlafly work so hard to defeat the Nineteenth Amendment? How might history have been different if she had failed?

- Why would a group that works for equality be unwelcoming toward certain groups of people?

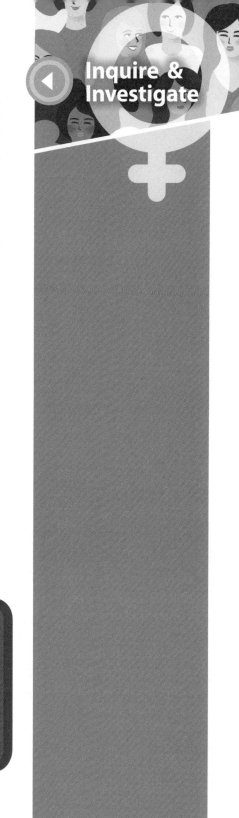

THE ELEMENTS OF THE SECOND WAVE

What elements made up second-wave feminism? Are we still struggling with some of these issues? How have they changed? How are they similar?

- **Do some research online or at the library on one of the more prominent issues of second-wave feminism.**

  - Which elements do you see as still relevant today?

  - Has this issue been solved? Yes? No? Partially?

  - Has this issue changed since people were discussing it during the 1960s and 1970s?

- **Look for images about your issue from the 1960s and 1970s and compare them with images about the same issues that have been published more recently.**

  - How are they different?

  - Has the tone of the issue as seen through images changed?

> **To investigate more,** find images from other countries that are connected to the issue you are researching. What are the laws surrounding that issue in those countries? What are the attitudes about the issue? How are they different from those attitudes in the United States?

QUOTE THAT!

Shirley Chisholm is an icon and pioneer as the first black female congresswoman. She is also an often-quoted source of wisdom. You'll find a list of her quotes below. What wisdom can you find in them today?

- **Read each quote.** What does it mean? Do you think the meaning of that quote has changed from the 1960s and '70s to today?

- **Research each quote at the library or on the internet.** When did Shirley say it? What was the circumstance? Did she ever say anything that conflicted with that quote?

  - "You don't make progress by standing on the sidelines, whimpering and complaining. You make progress by implementing ideas."

  - "The emotional, sexual, and psychological stereotyping of females begins when the doctor says, 'It's a girl.'"

  - "In the end, anti-black, anti-female, and all forms of discrimination are equivalent to the same thing—anti-humanism."

  - "When morality comes up against profit, it is seldom that profit loses."

  - "Tremendous amounts of talent are lost to our society just because that talent wears a skirt."

  - "At present, our country needs women's idealism and determination, perhaps more in politics than anywhere else."

To investigate more, consider what feminists today are saying that might be remembered decades from now. Read speeches or listen to videos of women speaking out about feminist issues. How are their quotes different from Shirley's? How are they similar? Why?

Chapter 5
Backlash

NOT EVERYONE WAS ON OUR SIDE.

Why did people think feminism had failed by the 1980s?

In the 1980s, many groups were saying the age of feminism was over, that women were more interested in their individual success. Some activists called this a backlash and showed that feminists were still working hard for change.

Although great strides were made during the second wave of feminism, they came at a price. Backlash is a strong, negative reaction that people feel and act on—especially when the reaction is to a social or political development. You might think that all people would appreciate equality among genders and greater empowerment for women, but as people realized during the 1980s and 1990s, this wasn't the case.

It seems that for every two steps feminism took forward, it took one step back. While the 1960s and 1970s were a period of activism and cultural revolution in the United States, during the 1980s, a shift occurred from looking outward toward looking inward. Many women refocused their energy on their personal goals.

What was wrong with this? There's nothing wrong in focusing on one's own future and working toward personal success. But no one exists in a vacuum. The issues that feminists had been striving to solve weren't going away on their own.

HAVING IT ALL

Have you heard the term, "having it all?" This was a popular concept in the 1980s. Many women believed the time was right for them to have it all—partners, children, meaningful work, and financial independence. They felt they were no longer constrained by the cultural and societal limitations that had affected their mothers and grandmothers. Feminism had finally won! Or had it?

What did having it all really look like? We can see some examples from movies of the time. According to the 1987 comedy *Baby Boom,* having it all meant having a baby, a lucrative job where you worked your own hours, and a great boyfriend. Remember the movie *Ferris Bueller's Day Off?* While Ferris was touring Chicago with his friends, his mother was at work, fielding calls from her children, and coming home to a supportive husband and beautiful house at the end of the day. She had it all, even as the wool was being pulled over her eyes by her mischievous and very funny son.

> Movies such as these showed the kind of life many women aspired to and believed achievable.

Unfortunately, in real life, very few women had the means to live this kind of a fantastical life. Although the 1980s saw increases in women's wages, they never reached anywhere near the level of what men were being paid for the same jobs. Women who weren't wealthy, especially single mothers, still had to figure out how to earn enough to feed their families and to pay for childcare while they worked. The ERA had not passed, and women were still struggling.

FEMINISM AROUND THE GLOBE

By the late 1970s and early 1980s, women's liberation movements in most European countries became less active and visible in response to the same anti-feminist backlash that the United States was experiencing. In England, activists were moving from direct action to finding ways to work with government agencies, while in the Netherlands, they worked to change laws that affected women's rights. Spanish feminists began to move into political organizations so that they could influence change. In Switzerland, feminist activists focused on violence against women and providing counseling services to abused women. The work to improve the lives of women continued, but in a less public way.[1]

You might think that as first prime minister of Britain, Margaret Thatcher (1925–2013) would symbolize feminism and women's progress. But the "Iron Lady," as she was nicknamed, did not promote women's causes.[11] What do you think of successful women like her?

While having it all sounded great, in reality most women constantly struggled to meet the conflicting demands of work, family, and self. Some felt doomed to fail, and the seeds of a backlash were planted.

WOMEN'S HEALTH

As women found fulfillment beyond the suburban homes that had represented happiness in the 1950s, they met many roadblocks. For example, their health and reproductive freedoms were threatened as *Roe v. Wade* came under attack. Some abortion clinics were bombed, often by people acting on behalf of extreme religious groups. Doctors, nurses, and people who worked at abortion clinics were sometimes shot at or attacked. Even without such violence, anti-abortion demonstrations outside the clinic doors made getting an abortion mentally, if not physically, risky.

You can see the variations in the levels of support for *Roe v. Wade*

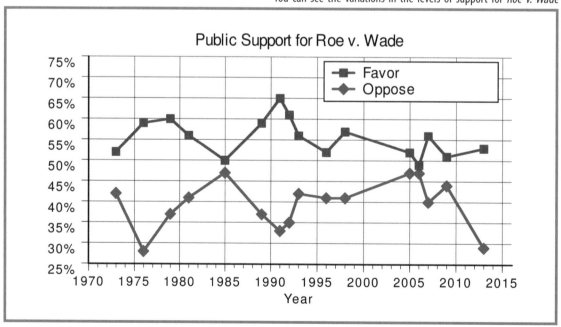

What did this have to do with feminism? One thing women want is access to health care, and if the places where they are seeking health care are being threatened, women's health is being threatened, too. Attacks on the places and people who are providing care, especially care that is controversial, can make it far more difficult and even impossible for women to access the care they need and have a right to.

Roe v. Wade continued to be put to the test through a series of Supreme Court decisions that gradually changed the law to add more restrictions. In terms of women's health, the 1980s was a time of struggle and setbacks that are still argued about today.

CULTURE WARS

Feminism was also argued about in the culture wars of the 1990s. The culture wars focused on issues that were believed to affect the moral direction of the country.

BABY BOOMERS

Baby boomers are people born between 1946 and 1964, a "boom time" for the American economy, and a popular time to raise a family. From the 1960s through the 1990s, baby boomers flooded the work place—including women. According to the Bureau of Labor Statistics, women's participation in the labor force peaked in 1999 and has gradually declined since.

Abortion protests are still common across the United States.

credit: Brian Stansberry (CC BY 3.0)

Abortion, privacy, homosexuality, and censorship were all issues being hotly debated by people on both sides of a wide gap in beliefs—in the media and by politicians. Some people, such as evangelist Jerry Falwell (1933–2007), organized themselves politically and led the charge. Jerry gained a wide audience by establishing an organization called the Moral Majority, a lobby group that was opposed to much of what feminists had fought to accomplish in the previous decades.

Some politicians and commentators believed that the culture wars divide broke along the lines of those who lived in rural settings, who were usually more conservative in their beliefs, and those who lived in cities, where a more liberal attitude reigned. As with all issues, it was more complex than that, but the result was a country deeply divided in its ideological views.

BACKLASH AND *BACKLASH*

Had the feminist movement failed? Sure, women had the right to vote, the right to choose, and the right to work, but was feminism itself a success?

Many women who were struggling with having it all were saying no. In 1992, 39 percent of women surveyed by *Redbook*, a top women's magazine, said that feminism had made it harder for women to balance work and family life.

A decade after the ERA failed to pass, *Atlantic* magazine found that the country was still ambivalent about woman's equality.

The proof of this ambivalence showed up regularly in the courts, especially the U.S. Supreme Court. Feminist writer Wendy Kaminer (1949–) noted, "The Court has not extended to women the same constitutional protection it has extended to racial minorities, because a majority of justices have never rejected the notion that some degree of sex discrimination is only natural." This is something that women continue to fight today.

In a 1993 article called "Feminism's Identity Crisis: The Most Effective Backlash Against Feminism Comes from Within," Wendy found that while most women said feminism had made their lives better, most of them also hesitated to identify as a feminist.

Feminists were often seen as strident, angry, and aggressive. Many women didn't want to be seen this way, even as they strongly believed in feminist ideas. Why do you think so many people associated these characteristics with feminists?

> Author Susan Faludi (1959–) thought the idea that feminism had failed was a backlash against the strides women had made for the last several decades.

She was inspired to write her 1991 book, *Backlash: The Undeclared War Against Women*, as a response to a 1986 story in *Newsweek* magazine called "Too Late for Prince Charming?" This story claimed that marriage prospects for single, educated professional women were at an all-time low. The authors of the article used statistics from a study by Harvard and Yale that were later found to be wrong, but the headline and the content were powerful enough that many people saw it as an end of feminism.

THE POWER OF WORDS

Susan Faludi uses the word *hysteria* to describe the way the media spread unfounded tales of the failure of feminism. Hysteria is a very important word in women's history, as it was used for decades to diagnosis women's physical and emotional complaints. It played into the myth that men were rational beings, while women were out of control with emotion because of their biological makeup. Can you think of other words that have been applied to one gender and not the other? Why do you think this happens?

If there was one word that captured the essence of feminism in the 1990s, it was contradiction. What do you see as some of the contradictions of this era?

In her book, Susan questioned the truth, accuracy, and motivation behind the article. Why were women being portrayed as needing to marry? Why were they pitied for not being able to find partners? She believed that women were being gaslighted about the failure of feminism.

In her introduction to *Backlash*, Susan wrote:

> "*The New York Times* reports: Childless women are 'depressed and confused' and their ranks are swelling. *Newsweek* says: Unwed women are 'hysterical' and crumbling under a 'profound crisis of confidence.'"

Susan also noted that the media used a lot of ink to report about a so-called "man shortage" that single women were struggling with. She asked if these headlines reflected reality and made it clear that mainstream media outlets were deliberately using made-up statistics to spread lies.

ON THE STAND

Susan Faludi's book became a worldwide bestseller and received a wealth of media coverage. It benefitted from timing, as the book's publication happened the same year as Anita Hill's (1956–) testimony during Clarence Thomas's (1948–) U.S. Supreme Court confirmation hearings. The hearings became one of the defining feminist moments of the 1990s.

In 1991, President George H.W. Bush (1924–2018) nominated federal circuit court Judge Clarence Thomas to replace Thurgood Marshall (1908–1993) on the Supreme Court. Justice Marshall was the country's first African American to serve on the Supreme Court. Clarence Thomas is also an African American, and a Republican.

SO, WE HAVE TO LIVE WITHIN THESE BROKEN SYSTEMS.

BUT THAT CAN BE A POWERFUL MOTIVATOR

RIGHT—NOW WE KNOW WHAT NEEDS TO CHANGE!

SO MUCH GOOD HAS COME FROM FOLKS REALIZING THEY'RE UNCOMFORTABLE—AND DON'T HAVE TO BE!

Although many Republicans are moderate, meaning they hold values that Democrats also share, Justice Thomas is not moderate. His politics and his history on the bench showed that he was a conservative, including being strongly against affirmative action.[4]

Affirmative action is a way of supporting members of populations who have historically been discriminated against, such as African Americans and women. For example, by following an affirmative action plan, a university might agree to accept a certain number of black applicants or a company might hire a certain number of women. This helps ensure that institutional discrimination— discrimination that exists within an organization— doesn't grow and spread.

> Before joining the Supreme Court, nominees must go through a confirmation hearing to ensure that they are suitable for the job.

FEMINIST FACT

It might seem ironic that President George H.W. Bush backed a federal bill against sexual harassment that Congress passed in 1995. Within a year, the courts were inundated with claims by women seeking justice.

During Clarence Thomas's confirmation hearings, a scandal erupted. A former employee, Anita Hill, came forward and accused him of sexually harassing her when she worked for him at the Department of Education and the Equal Employment Opportunity Commission. She had given testimony privately to the FBI, but the story had leaked and she was called to appear at the hearings. These took place in October 1991 and were televised.

> The country was glued to their televisions as the hearings took center stage.

Anita Hill, also African American, was a respected law professor. Her decorum in front of the camera was the opposite of a vindictive feminist liar trying to topple a powerful man, which was how Republican and even some Democratic senators portrayed her.

She never wavered in her testimony and reported that Clarence asked her out on dates, even when she repeatedly declined. She also testified that he persisted in discussing graphic sexual matters with her at the office.

Anita even passed a polygraph test. Clarence, on the other hand, refused to take such a test. Although this raised some eyebrows, Anita was still vilified. Some people claimed that her entire story was made up by white liberals who did not want to see a black conservative on the Supreme Court.

Ultimately, even though the country and the committee were divided on the controversy, Clarence Thomas was confirmed to the Supreme Court by a narrow margin. What did this show people who supported Anita Hill? What did this say to women who had been sexually harassed in their lifetimes?

Anita Hill went on to publish, teach, speak, and lead a life as a great example of a well-respected warrior for women's rights and social justice.

She became a key figure again during Brett Kavanaugh's (1965–) Supreme Court confirmation hearings in 2018. Brett Kavanaugh is a Republican who was nominated to the Supreme Court by President Donald Trump.

During the confirmation hearings, three women accused Justice Kavanaugh of sexual misconduct. One of those women—Dr. Christine Blasey Ford—was called to testify. The slogan, "I Believe Anita Hill," went viral on social media as the country once again watched a woman describe her experience of being sexually harassed by a proposed justice. Despite Christine's testimony, Brett Kavanaugh was confirmed to the Supreme Court soon after the hearings.

Although, Anita Hill's fight failed to disqualify Clarence Thomas for the Supreme Court, 1992 was deemed "The Year of the Woman" because four women were elected to the U.S. Senate in one year, an unprecedented event. But would things change in more than a token fashion? For every "year of the woman," would another backlash brew?

TASLIMA NASRIN

Taslima Nasrin (1962–) is a feminist author who was born in East Pakistan (now Bangladesh). In articles, novels, and poems, she forcefully criticized the Islamic code that she believed turned women into the property of men. Her criticism and outspokenness offended strict Muslims, as did her short hair and refusal to wear traditional Muslim dress. Taslima's suggestion that the Koran—the Islamic sacred book—should be revised led to cries for her death. She went into exile in Sweden in 1994 before moving to India in 2004. But once again, Islamists forced her to flee—this time to America. Throughout this, she continued to write, publishing her autobiography, novels, and poetry.[5]

KEY QUESTIONS

- **Why might women change their focus from themselves as a group to themselves as individuals? What made this possible?**

- **Can you think of examples of backlash in other areas? What about the African American experience? What about immigration?**

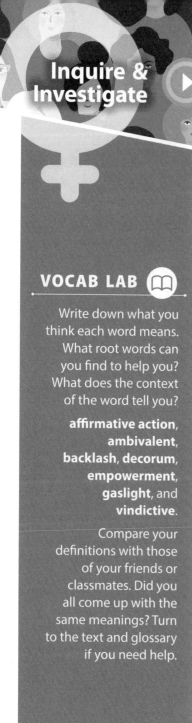

MEDIA AND THE BACKLASH

Often, we can use popular media of a certain period to explore different issues. How do movies, television shows, and books reflect what's going on in the real world? How do they show what's going on with feminist issues?

- **Watch kids' movies from the 1980s and 1990s.** Even movies that you've watched before can reveal surprising things if you keep in mind the following questions.

  - How are women portrayed in these movies?

  - What roles do the mothers play? Sisters? Female friends?

  - How many movies have a girl or woman as a main character?

- **Read books that were popular in the 1980s and 1990s.** Consider the characters and plots while keeping the previous questions in mind.

- **Compare the books you read and movies you watched to those you read and watch that are made in your own time.** Are they different (besides the special effects!)? How? Are female characters more present and active today than they were in earlier decades? Have portrayals of men and women changed? How? Why?

> **To investigate more,** choose several pieces of media from different decades. Watch the shows with a friend or classmate and have them guess which decade the show was from. How can they tell?

VOCAB LAB

Write down what you think each word means. What root words can you find to help you? What does the context of the word tell you?

affirmative action, **ambivalent**, **backlash**, **decorum**, **empowerment**, **gaslight**, and **vindictive**.

Compare your definitions with those of your friends or classmates. Did you all come up with the same meanings? Turn to the text and glossary if you need help.

Chapter 6 ▶
The Third Wave

FEMINISM ISN'T JUST ABOUT **SOME** WOMEN, IT'S ABOUT **ALL** WOMEN.

Why should feminism encompass the needs of all women?

Intersectionality is the idea that all women, including women of color, lesbians, and transgender women, should be considered part of the movement for equal rights and representation. When all people are lifted up, everyone benefits.

When feminism first emerged in the nineteenth century, the United States was ruled by a mostly white, male, Christian majority. As the twentieth century drew to a close and the twenty-first century began, a shift occurred. With help from the internet, a wave of globalism began to spread across the world. People living on all sides of the planet could communicate with each other easily. Schools, the media, and society itself began to recognize the value of multiculturalism.

It became clear that in order to compete in a global economy, young people would be at an advantage if they were well-traveled, well-educated, and well-versed in the languages and cultures of other countries. Cultural barriers began to tumble, and the cultural makeup of the population in the United States shifted in many ways. Issues of diversity became part of the national conversation about feminism.

People began to recognize that all the progress that had been made so far would be felt more deeply and by more people with the inclusion of more groups of people. This is called intersectionality.

The idea behind intersectionality is to make feminism more inclusive so that it does not only reflect white, heterosexual, middle-class women. But it is an ever-changing concept, especially as some people are critical of the idea. We've seen how African Americans, lesbians, and transgender people were—or weren't—included in the first two waves of feminism. Now, let's look at how intersectionality began to develop in the last few years of the twentieth century.

WELCOME TO THE 1990S

In the 1990s, even with the backlash against feminism, the ideas of second-wave feminism continued to be put into practice. Women had more access to birth control and health care and had more control over their bodies. Laws against sexual harassment were on the books. It seemed as if progress was being made.

This was when many people began to better recognize that the feminist movement was made up of lots of different people with lots of different backgrounds and identities. Women of color, lesbians, transgender people—all of these groups were working toward gaining equality. Even though on the surface, some of the issues might seem quite different, the end goal tended to be the same—equality.

THE COMBAHEE RIVER COLLECTIVE

The early seeds of intersectionality were planted by a black, feminist, lesbian organization that was active in Boston, Massachusetts, in the late 1970s—the Combahee River Collective. Its collective statement, a key tool in the development of intersectionality, read, "We are a collective of Black feminists who have been meeting together since 1974 . . . while at the same time doing political work within our own group and in coalition with other progressive organizations and movements. The most general statement of our politics at the present time would be that we are actively committed to struggling against racial, sexual, heterosexual, and class oppression, and see as our particular task the development of integrated analysis and practice based upon the fact that the major systems of oppression are interlocking."[1]

View some of the Lesbian Herstory Archives at this website. Why is it important to keep historical records of populations that are often skipped over in history classes?

Lesbian Herstory

In 1992, Rebecca Walker (1969–), the daughter of Alice Walker (1944–), who wrote the novel *The Color Purple*, wrote an article for *Ms.* magazine in which she proclaimed, "I am the third wave." In it, she gave a passionate reaction to the Anita Hill hearings that we discussed in Chapter 5.

> Rebecca presented herself as a role model to intersectional feminists who wanted to expand their voices from anger and awareness into concrete action.

She vowed to hold her standards up to a feminist standard of justice, as her mother did before her, and to dedicate her life to female empowerment.

"To be a feminist," she wrote in her article, "is to integrate an ideology of equality and female empowerment into the very fiber of my life. It is to search for personal clarity in the midst of systemic destruction, to join in sisterhood with women when often we are divided, to understand power structures with the intention of challenging them."

Some of the women who might be considered part of the third wave of feminism were working on feminist issues all along. Lesbians first fought for visibility and acknowledgement within the second wave of feminism, but as years passed, they wanted to more thoroughly document their own experiences.

The Lesbian Herstory Archives were founded in New York City in 1974 by Joan Nestle (1940–) and some members of the Gay Academic Union. The founders wanted to preserve lesbian stories for future generations in the form of books, articles, pictures, memorabilia, and more.

Today, the archives include 11,000 books, 1,300 periodical titles, and an unknown number of photographs. It's a wealth of information and experience that people can look toward for guidance, reassurance, and community.

One thing feminism addresses is the need for all women to have a voice that's heard by the rest of society. The Lesbian Herstory Archives achieves this through its extensive collection.

FEMINISM AND TRANSGENDER PEOPLE

Another population that has long felt the need to be heard is the transgender community. Transgender is a term that includes people who don't conform to gender norms. Many trans people have a gender identity that is different from the physical sex they were assigned at birth. For example, someone who was assigned male at birth might discover they actually identify as a woman. Some people have a gender expression, such as clothes, make-up, or hair, that does not fit with traditional ideas of gender. Nonbinary people are people who don't identify with either gender. Because of this, many nonbinary people prefer "they" as their pronoun.

You might be wondering what this has to do with feminism. What happens when a transgender woman who was born as a male begins to take on the characteristics of and live as a female?

Should feminism include her?
Is she entitled to the same rights as a
woman who was born as a female?

CHUTNEY POPCORN

Nisha Ganatra (1974–) is a Canadian actor and director. Her 2000 breakthrough debut comedy, *Chutney Popcorn*, tells the story of a lesbian Indian girl who offers to serve as a surrogate mother for her sister, who can't have children. Nisha said in an interview, "I really wanted to make sure the movie was *not* about the Indian American experience and *not* about the gay and lesbian experience. The movie is about what this family goes through and what they do to stay together." What do Nisha's hopes for this movie show about the culture at large? Were lesbianism and multiculturalism becoming more mainstream in the early years of the twenty-first century?[2] Watch a clip of *Chutney Popcorn* at this website.

🔍 Chutney Popcorn trailer

Some feminists and groups have welcomed transgender people into their ranks, but some have disputed the notion that a transgender woman is a "real" woman. Transgender women have been excluded from many feminist gatherings.

The Transgender Pride Flag

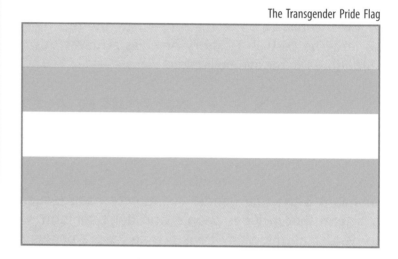

One example of this fissure in the feminist community can be found in the story of Sandy Stone (c. 1936–). Sandy is an American author, media theorist, and performance artist who has also worked as a recording engineer and computer programmer—among many other things. She is transgender and is considered the founder of the academic field of transgender studies.

While Sandy was a member of the Olivia Records collective, an all-female music recording company, an incident occurred that illustrates the divide that sometimes exists between transgender women and feminists. In 1979, Janice Raymond (1943–), a radical, lesbian feminist, wrote the book, *The Transsexual Empire: The Making of the She-Male*, in which she accused Sandy of trying to destroy Olivia Records and womanhood in general with "male energy."

Janice quoted one woman as saying, "I feel raped when Olivia passes off Sandy . . . as a real woman. After all his male privilege, is he going to cash in on lesbian feminist culture too?" Although the collective defended Sandy, the threat of a boycott led her to leave it.

In 1983, Sandy published the essay, "The Empire Strikes Back: A Posttranssexual Manifesto." A key point that the essay makes is that transgender people should come out and not hide who they are—that doing so leads to empowerment. Sandy's essay was highly influential and encouraged transgender people to assert themselves in often "unwelcoming" environments. The essay is considered a foundational work in transgender research and has been translated into many languages.[3]

Even as transgender issues come more to the forefront of the feminist movement, plenty of fear continues to exist. Many in our society still consider transgender people to be outside the experience of most of the population, and fear of those unlike us has always inspired disruption and even violence. We can see this fear playing out politically in the debate over bathrooms.

THE BATHROOM WARS

Some of the issues that have arisen during the third wave of feminism might not seem like feminist issues on the surface. One example of this is the "bathroom wars." Have you heard this term?

The bathroom wars have become a symbol of the political and social struggles faced by transgender people. How is this a feminist issue?

Did you know that in Rwanda, women hold 64 percent of the seats in the national legislature (equivalent to the U.S. Congress)—the largest share of any country? But the roles of women and men remain complicated. Women may have powerful roles in public, but this power doesn't translate into their own homes. They are still expected to perform traditional—and sometimes menial—domestic duties. Feminism itself is viewed as Western and "not Rwandan." Learn more about women in Rwanda and the story of Mireille Umutoni Sekamana and her incredible debate team.

NPR Rwanda debate team

As more and more feminists embrace intersectionality, they widen their focus to include the issues faced by all women, including transgender women. In this way, the bathroom wars are a concern for all feminists.

The bathroom wars started in 2012 when college campuses, and a growing number of high schools, installed gender-neutral bathrooms that everyone could use, regardless of their gender. Why was this important for people who, for example, identify as female yet have male genitalia? It gave them a place where they could be private and safe.

A year later, Texas and several other states introduced "bathroom surveillance" bills that would require transgender people to use bathrooms that matched the gender on their birth certificates. Many in the transgender community saw this as a backlash against the gains they had made in being recognized as full citizens deserving of equal rights.

> People who supported these bills claimed they were trying to protect women and children from men who might pretend to be transgender in order to get into a women's bathroom.

At the end of 2015, the state of Washington had clarified that existing law allowed transgender people to use bathrooms consistent with their gender identity. Other states followed suit. In February 2016, the people of Charlotte, North Carolina, passed a new law that allowed transgender people to use bathrooms that match their gender identity.

PEOPLE ARE GETTING SO UPSET OVER... BATHROOMS?

WHEN I GO TO THE BATHROOM, THAT'S ALL I WANT TO DO—

GO TO THE BATHROOM.

THAT'S ALL ANY OF US WANT!

But in March of that year, the North Carolina governor, Pat McCrory (1956–), signed a bill called HB 2 into law, which struck down all existing LGBTQ nondiscrimination laws across the state. It banned transgender people from using some public restrooms.

> The bill was swept through the legislative process and signed by the governor at such speed that some lawmakers claimed they didn't even have a chance to read it.

A year later, the law was repealed. As many powerful individuals and organizations protested HB 2 by canceling events and closing businesses, the state government made moves to fix the issue. However, the repeal of the law didn't further the rights of the LGBTQ population, it only returned rights that had been taken from them by HB 2.

FEMINIST FACT

TERF stands for trans exclusionary radical feminist. Transgender advocates use this term to describe feminists who are against including transgender women in female spaces and organizations because they were assigned male—not female—at birth. But those who are called TERFs see it as a slur.[4]

Then U.S. Attorney General Loretta Lynch (1959–) weighed in when she spoke about transgender rights.

> "What we must not do—what we must never do—is turn on our neighbors, our family members, our fellow Americans, for something they cannot control, and deny what makes them human. This is why none of us can stand by when a state enters the business of legislating identity and insists that a person pretend to be something they are not, or invents a problem that doesn't exist as a pretext for discrimination and harassment."[5]

As transgender people, homosexuals, and people of color gain more visibility and different movements join together to share power, the future of feminism might look much different from the waves that have come in the past.

What do you think it will mean to be a feminist as the twenty-first century grows older?

WOMEN'S RIGHTS ARE HUMAN RIGHTS

On September 5, 1995, in Beijing, China, Hillary Rodham Clinton (1947–), then first lady, gave a speech to the UN 4th World Conference on Women in which she stated, "The great challenge of this conference is to give voice to women everywhere whose experiences go unnoticed, whose words go unheard. Women comprise more than half the world's population, 70 percent of the world's poor, and two-thirds of those who are not taught to read and write." Read the transcript of her speech at this website. How can people around the world work together to improve the lives of all women?

🔍 American Rhetoric Hilary Clinton

KEY QUESTIONS

- Why does it matter if movements are made up of more than one demographic? How are they made stronger when people representing different experiences, identities, and backgrounds work together?

- The year 2018 saw a great increase in transgender political candidates. Do you think that being openly transgender is simply becoming more acceptable? Do you think this might be the precursor of a backlash?

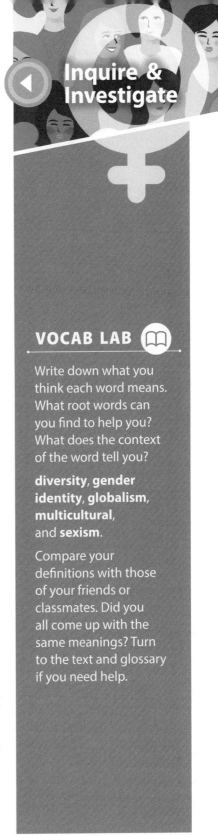

INTERSECTIONALITY IN FILMS, TV, AND OTHER MEDIA

What might the first wave of feminism have been like if Alice Paul and her cohorts had access to the internet? The suffragists might have been a YouTube sensation! We live in a much more sensory and media-driven world than the early feminists did. What does this mean for the feminist movement?

- **Use your skills as a twenty-first century journalist.** Track down film clips, music videos, speeches, podcasts, and blogs that illustrate third-wave feminism.

  - Who do you think best expresses the goals of intersectionality?

  - If you had to come up with a concise slogan to embody the goals of intersectionality, what would it be?

  - How does intersectionality relate to your world and your peers' world today?

- **Share your research with friends and classmates.** What are their experiences with intersectionality?

VOCAB LAB

Write down what you think each word means. What root words can you find to help you? What does the context of the word tell you?

diversity, gender identity, globalism, multicultural, and **sexism**.

Compare your definitions with those of your friends or classmates. Did you all come up with the same meanings? Turn to the text and glossary if you need help.

> **To investigate more,** explain intersectional feminism to someone older than yourself and note what they find fascinating or confusing or both. Do the same with a younger person. What were the similarities? How were the two responses different? What does this show about a changing society?

THE RAINBOW WAVE

As we've discussed, when more women are elected to positions of political power, more change can be seen in terms of equal rights for women. The same holds true for trans women. The year 2018 saw several trans women elected into political positions. Do some research and make some predictions about how these women could change the political, cultural, and legal landscape for all.

- **At the library or on the internet, research a few of the following trans women.**

  - Danica Roem
  - Andrea Jenkins
  - Kim Coco Iwamoto
  - Christine Hallquist
  - Alexandra Chandler
  - Amelia Marquez
  - Melissa Sklarz

- **As you read about them, ask yourself the following questions.**

  - Do the candidates feel that being transgendered affects their political careers or outlooks? If so, how?

  - Are the candidates more liberal or conservative? Can you find any patterns?

  - Why is it crucial to have people with different backgrounds serving as politicians and lawmakers?

- **Prepare a presentation of one of the people you researched and present what you have learned to your class or family.** What kinds of questions do people have about the person you chose? Do you think more transgender people will run for office in the near future?

To investigate further, find transgender politicians from other countries and research their political careers. Is there anything different about their experiences compared to how people campaign, vote, and govern in the United States?

Chapter 7
Feminism Today

What are women's lives like today?

Just as we saw in the 1980s, something of a backlash is happening against feminism today. After nearly seeing the first female president elected in the United States in 2016, the country has instead watched as laws that protect the rights of women and other minorities have been chipped away. In response, many people are becoming more involved in activism.

On January 21, 2017, a worldwide women's march took place. It was possibly the largest march in U.S. history.[1] Just a day after the inauguration of President Donald Trump, about 4 million people marched in the United States, many of them braving harsh winter weather. More than 100,000 people gathered in Washington, DC.

What were they protesting? Why did so many people feel compelled to peacefully take to the streets, hold signs, and wear pink hats?

In 2016, many people felt that the country, and indeed much of the world, was taking huge steps backward in time to an earlier era before the women's movement and the LGBTQ movement had improved the lives of so many. People were concerned that the strides the feminism movement had made in terms of health care, pay equity, and a culture of respect were being chipped away.

A scene from the 2017 women's march

credit: VeryBusyPeople (CC BY 2.0)

The women's march was in large part a reaction to the inauguration of Donald Trump as president of the United States.

Donald Trump's presidential campaign was fraught with controversy over demeaning remarks he'd made about women. Plus, he had expressed support for legislation that affected women's access to health care, including threatening to dismantle *Roe v. Wade*, the Supreme Court decision that made abortion legal. In addition, Vice President Mike Pence (1959–) was known for being against Planned Parenthood, a health care organization that provides care to millions to American women, including access to safe birth control and abortions.[2]

FEMINIST FACT

Women still do not always get paid as much as men for the same work. In 2017, women earned 82 percent of what men earned. This is an ongoing challenge for women.

Many women were scared and angry. The march captured the energy of the moment and came together as an effort to advocate for women's rights, LGBTQ rights, racial equality, immigration reform, and more.

But the march, while giving people an outlet to express their support of each other and of a shared value system that saw all people as equals, didn't change the fact that people in positions of power did not share those values.

#METOO MOVEMENT

So how did the energy seen during the women's march affect feminism in the second decade of the twenty-first century? For one thing, many women decided it was time to speak up more.

In October 2017, the #MeToo movement was sparked on various social media platforms. Women from around the world chimed in and shared their experiences of being sexually harassed or assaulted. Many others expressed support of the people who were telling their stories.

Why did this happen? The #MeToo movement corresponded to the sexual harassment charges brought against several prominent figures in politics, business, and the entertainment industry. These included charges made against well-known, powerful men such as Harvey Weinstein, Roger Ailes, Charlie Rose, and James Levine. As the news stories about these men unfolded, more and more allegations against others came to light.

Sometimes, people talk about a "glass ceiling" that prevents women from advancing in their jobs. They can see what success might look like, but they can't break through the invisible barrier to achieve it.

Women saw an opportunity to express solidarity with those who were speaking up about their harrowing experiences, even at the risk of being mocked, threatened, or not believed. The #MeToo movement was born.

The #MeToo movement has shown that women continue to face sexual harassment in their daily lives, which can affect their emotional health, their ability to advance in their careers, and where they feel safe. The feminist movement still has work to do to make the world a safer place for women.

How are women doing in other areas? How far have they come since colonial times? Let's take a look.

LEARNING, WORKING, LEADING

Girls and women in the United States have come a very long way from the days when they received little to no education. According to the National Center for Education Statistics, in the fall of 2018, females were expected to account for the majority of college students—11.2 million females compared to 8.7 million males. Women also earn a significant portion of graduate degrees in fields such as medicine and law.

It's terrific news that so many women are getting the education they want. However, colleges would like to see more balance. Perhaps the ratio is a kind of backlash from the years when women were discouraged from pursuing an education.

You probably know many women who work, from your own mother to the doctor you see to the pilot on a plane you take. Many more job opportunities are open today to women than even 50 years ago. In the corporate world, however, few women advance to the jobs at the highest levels.

SONYA SOTOMAYOR

Sonia Sotomayor is a woman who serves as a role model to many. She is the first Hispanic and the third woman to serve on the U.S. Supreme Court. She was appointed by President Barack Obama in 2009. Born in 1954, Sonia came from humble beginnings. Raised in one of the poorest areas of New York City, the South Bronx, Sonia faced many obstacles. Her father died from heart complications when she was nine, leaving her to be raised by her single mom, a nurse. Sonia pursued a career in the law and attended Yale Law School, one of the most prestigious law schools in the country. She has distinguished herself by writing bold dissents against majority rulings on issues that matter to her involving racial justice and justice for women.

As of 2018, only 25 women were CEOs of Fortune 500 companies, which are considered the largest companies. They included Mary Barra of General Motors, Ginny Rometty of IBM, and Beth Ford of Land O'Lakes.

What about the government? Have women made any headway in politics? After all, it's the people we elect who make and change the laws.

Large numbers of women ran for office and voted in the November 2018 mid-term elections. The results were many "firsts": Ayanna Pressley (1974–) is Massachusetts' first African American, female member of Congress; Rashida Tlaib (1976–) from Michigan and Ilhan Omar (1982–) from Minnesota are the first two Muslim women to serve in Congress; and Sharice Davids from Kansas is the first lesbian Native American to serve. Alexandria Ocasio-Cortez (1989–) of New York is the youngest female ever to be elected to Congress.

Women continue to march in a quest to protect their rights.

credit: Fibonacci Blue, St. Paul, Minnesota (CC BY 2.0)

POP CULTURE

As we saw in Chapter 5, popular culture can be an indicator of how society values different groups of people. What musical artists do you listen to? Who is starring in the movies you go to see? Do you see characters who look like you and share your qualities on the big screen?

> As the 2010s wound down, more and more women were making their mark in mainstream pop culture.

Films such as *Wonder Woman* and *A Wrinkle in Time* included strong female leads. In pop music, Beyoncé even performed onstage in 2016 in front of giant lights outlining the word "feminist." However, some people feel that performers such as Beyoncé actually do a disservice to feminism because of the way they dress and the way they dance. What do you think?

Remember reading about the early history of women and seeing that there were not many female writers and artists? That's changed! Now you can go into almost any bookstore or library or museum and find work done by women. Tomi Adeyemi (1993–) wrote a fantasy book called *Children of Blood and Bone* that met rave reviews from both critics and teens when it was published in 2018. Angie Thomas (1988–) stunned readers with her depiction of the aftermath of a race-related shooting in her 2018 book, *The Hate U Give*.

These women are standing on the mountain of work that came before them, work done by feminists of the 1800s, 1900s, and early twenty-first century, who struggled and fought so that women would have the chance to be considered equal.

GLOBAL FEMINISM: MATERNITY LEAVE

One feminist issue is that of maternity leave, or the time a person is allowed to take from work after having a baby. This is called paternity leave when it's the father taking the time. Countries vary widely in terms of what is offered for maternity leave, both in the length of the leave and what the person can expect to collect in wages while they are at home with the baby. If you've just had a baby, you might want to be living in Latvia, where you get 112 days and 100 percent of your wages, or even Japan, where you get 14 weeks at 67 percent of your wages. You might not want to be in the United States, where you get three months and there's no federal law saying you need to be paid at all—it's up to your state or employer!

To hear Emma Gonzalez speak about gun violence, visit this website. Why might gun violence be considered a feminist issue?

Variety Emma Gonzalez

While their accomplishments are to be celebrated, there is still work to be done. In the arts, sciences, academics, business, and politics, women are still being paid less than men. Women are still being excluded from certain arenas, whether intentionally or inadvertently. What else can the feminist movement do?

STAY-AT-HOME PARENTS

Remember how in the 1950s, most women stayed home raising children and taking care of household tasks? Today, while women are still more likely than men to stay at home to raise their children, an increasing number of men are "stay-at-home" dads. The U.S. Census Bureau doesn't track people by this category, so exact numbers are hard to find.

Why is the number of stay-at-home dads rising? Sometimes, their wives have high-paying jobs and want to pursue their career goals. But many men just want to be more involved in raising their kids.[5] Do you know any stay-at-home dads?

You may be surprised to learn that a 2013 Pew survey found that 51 percent of respondents believed that children were better off with stay-at-home mothers and only 8 percent believed they were better off with stay-at-home fathers.[6] Why do you think this might be?

THE FUTURE IS YOU

All change starts with the individual and spreads out from there. For example, when a mass shooting took place at Marjory Stoneman Douglas High School in Parkland, Florida, student Emma Gonzalez became a national spokeswoman about gun violence.

If feminism is about inclusion of all voices, Emma Gonzalez embodies the courage of feminist convictions.

Born in 1997, Malala Yousafzai has long advocated for education for girls. In fact, her work made her the youngest person in history to receive the Nobel Peace Prize. While an adolescent in Pakistan, she blogged about what it was like to be a teenage girl under Taliban rule. Her outspokenness led to an assassination attempt that almost took her life.

> She recovered and went on to become an international speaker and found the Malala Fund, which sponsors schools for girls who normally would not receive an education because of gender discrimination.

Things can change in the blink of an eye in this country and in the world. Sisterhood is powerful, and it includes brothers in the fight. The fight for women's rights has been going on for centuries, but it is far from over.

What can you do to change the world?

VOCAB LAB

Write down what you think each word means. What root words can you find to help you? What does the context of the word tell you?

maternity leave, **popular culture**, and **sexual harassment**.

Compare your definitions with those of your friends or classmates. Did you all come up with the same meanings? Turn to the text and glossary if you need help.

KEY QUESTIONS

- What are some things you can do to make feminism more a part of your life?
- Why is it important for everyone, not just women, to work together for women's rights?
- How has feminism changed from the first wave of suffragists to today?

GLOBAL FEMINISM

Global feminism addresses women's rights across all nations, not just the United States. We've explored how feminism developed in the United States. How does American feminism compare to that of feminism in other countries?

- **Choose three countries to research how women are treated there today.** What are their daily lives like? What issues matter most to them? Make three columns and list the issues of feminism for each country.

- **How do the issues in these countries compare to the issues in the United States?** Are the goals of feminism similar across the world? What's different?

- **Make a Venn diagram and discover the overlapping issues among the countries.** You can make a Venn diagram by drawing three overlapping circles and listing the feminist issues of each country within a circle. The overlapping issues go in the overlapping spaces.

- **Did any of your research surprise you?** Why?

To investigate more, find blogs, podcasts, or other media being created by young people in countries outside the United States. How are their lives different from yours? How do your needs and goals resemble each other? Why is it important to explore the values and ways of other places?

abbess: the person in charge of a convent.

abolish: get rid of.

abolitionist: a person who supported ending slavery.

abortion: the ending of pregnancy by removing an embryo or fetus before it can survive outside the uterus.

activism: working to create social change.

activist: a person who works for social or political change.

adultery: the unfaithfulness of a married person to his or her spouse.

affirmative action: a policy or practice that seeks to improve employment and education opportunities for people who have been historically discriminated against.

alienate: to cause someone to feel isolated.

alimony: money paid to a spouse after a divorce.

allegation: an accusation of wrongdoing.

ally: a loyal friend who supports a cause.

ambivalent: having mixed feelings or contradictory ideas about something or someone.

architect: a person who designs buildings.

astronomer: a person who studies the stars, planets, and other objects in space.

baby boom: a temporary marked increase in the birth rate, especially the one following World War II.

backlash: a strong negative reaction.

bankrupt: to be unable to repay debts.

BCE: put after a date, BCE stands for Before Common Era and counts down to zero. CE stands for Common Era and counts up from zero. These non-religious terms correspond to BC and AD. This book was printed in 2019 CE.

benefactor: someone or something that provides help or an advantage.

birth control: a way to prevent pregnancy. Also called contraception.

bisexual: sexually attracted to both men and women.

bootleg: illegal liquor.

boycott: to stop buying a product or using a service as a way to protest something.

capitalism: an economic system in which a country's trade and industry are controlled by private individuals and operated for profit.

catalyst: an event or person who causes a change.

census: an official count or survey of a population.

charity: help for people in need.

citizenship: legally belonging to a country and having the rights and protection of that country.

civil rights: the rights that every person should have regardless of gender, race, or religion.

climate change: changes in the earth's climate patterns, including rising temperatures, which is called global warming.

collaborate: to work with others.

consciousness-raising groups: when people gather in small groups to discuss feelings, needs, and desires as they work to find common ground.

conservative: holding to traditional attitudes and values and reluctant to change, especially about politics or religion.

constitution: a document containing a country's basic laws and governing principles.

contraception: strategies for preventing pregnancy.

controversy: something that causes a lot of argument or disagreement.

criteria: the standard by which something is judged or measured.

crusade: to organize a campaign concerning a political, social, or religious issue.

culture: the beliefs and way of life of a group of people.

culture jamming: a tactic used by some social movements to disrupt media.

culture wars: a conflict between those values considered traditionalist or conservative and those considered progressive or liberal.

GLOSSARY

decorum: proper, polite behavior.

decrypt: to decode a message.

degradation: the act of ruining or damaging something.

dialogue: a conversation between two people.

diplomacy: talks between countries to solve differences.

discrimination: the unfair treatment of a person or a group of people because of who they are.

disenfranchise: to deprive someone of a right or privilege.

diversity: a variety of people from different backgrounds.

domestic: within the home.

dowry: property or money brought by a bride to her husband on their marriage.

drought: a long period of time with little or no rain.

Dust Bowl: the region of the south central United States that was damaged in the 1920s and 1930s by persistent dust storms that killed off crops and livestock.

economic: having to do with the resources and wealth of a country.

election: a vote where citizens choose a leader.

empowerment: having authority and power.

enslaved: made a slave.

entitled: believing oneself to be inherently deserving of special treatment.

environmental: relating to the natural world and the impact of human activity on its condition.

Equal Rights Amendment (ERA): an amendment to the U.S. Constitution guaranteeing that rights apply equally to all people, regardless of their gender.

equality: having equal rights, opportunities, and status.

equity: fair; freedom from bias or favoritism.

ethnicity: a category of people who identify with each other based on common ancestry, language, history, culture, or nation of origin.

eugenics: the science of trying to improve a human population by controlled breeding.

evangelist: a person who seeks to convert others to the Christian faith.

exercising: using, wielding.

extremist: a person who holds extreme views and advocates for extreme action.

faction: a small, organized group within a larger group, party, government, or organization.

feminism: the theory of the political, economic, and social equality of the sexes.

feminist: a person who believes men and women should have equal rights and opportunities.

firestorm: something that is intense and easily flares up with emotion.

first-wave feminism: a period during the nineteenth and early twentieth centuries when the feminism movement focused on legal issues, primarily on gaining the right to vote.

flapper: a fashionable young woman in the 1920s who wore short skirts and a short hairstyle, listened to jazz, and often behaved in ways not considered acceptable at the time.

fleet: a group of ships.

frontier: the boundary or edge.

garner: to gather or collect.

gaslight: to make someone think what they know to be true is false.

gender: the behavioral, cultural, or psychological traits typically associated with masculinity and femininity.

gender identity: a person's internal sense of being male, female, some combination of male and female, or neither male nor female.

gender non-conforming: describes a person whose gender identity does not conform to the prevailing ideas or practices of gender.

genitalia: the external organs of the reproductive system, including the penis and vagina.

globalism: considering the world and its population as a whole.

Great Depression: the deepest and longest-lasting economic downturn in the history of the Western industrialized world. The Great Depression occurred between 1929 and 1939.

Harlem Renaissance: an intellectual, social, and artistic explosion that took place in Harlem, New York, during the 1920s.

heckle: to yell aggressive comments or abuse.

heir: a person who inherits a title or property from a parent.

heterosexual: a person who is sexually attracted to others of the opposite gender.

Hispanic: of or relating to the people, speech, or culture of Spain or a person of Latin American descent living in the United States.

homestead: the home and land of a family.

Homestead Act: an act passed by Congress in 1862 enabling people to settle on pieces of undeveloped land to gain title after living on and farming the land for five years.

homosexual: a person who is sexually attracted to others of the same gender.

human rights: the rights that belong to all people, such as freedom from torture, the right to live, and freedom from slavery.

hunger strike: a form of protest in which protesters refuse to eat until their demands have been met.

hysteria: exaggerated or uncontrollable emotion or excitement.

iconic: a widely recognized symbol of a certain time.

idealism: the practice of forming or pursuing ideals.

ideology: a set of opinions or beliefs.

immigration: moving to a new country to live there.

immoral: something that goes against what is generally accepted as moral, or right.

immunity: a natural resistance.

inequity: the fact of being unfair, or an unfair situation.

inferior: lower in rank or status or quality.

inhumane: without compassion for misery or suffering, cruel.

injustice: unfair action or treatment.

innate: inborn or natural.

intellectual: involving serious thought.

intersectionality: the complex way different forms of discrimination combine, overlap, and intersect.

ironic: an event or situation that is interesting and sometimes humorous because it is the opposite of what you would expect.

Jazz Age: a post-World War I movement during the 1920s, from which jazz music and dance emerged.

judicial: having to do with the branch of government that interprets laws and administers justice.

Latin: the language of ancient Rome and its empire.

leisure economy: a way of life that allows more time for rest, relaxation, and fun.

lesbian: a woman who is sexually attracted to women.

LGBTQ: stands for lesbian, gay, bisexual, transgender, and queer.

liberal: open to new behavior and opinions and willing to discard traditional values.

literate: having the ability to read.

lobby: to try to influence legislators on an issue.

lucrative: making a great deal of money or profit.

lyrical: artistically beautiful and expressive.

manipulation: cleverly and unfairly controlling or influencing a person or situation.

maternity leave: the time a mother is allowed to take from work after having a baby.

media savvy: having a shrewd understanding of how to deal with publicity and the media.

media: the industry in the business of presenting news to the public, by methods including radio, television, Internet, and newspapers.

memorabilia: items kept to remember someone by.

GLOSSARY

menial labor: boring work that does not require skill and pays very little money.

meter: rhythmic lines of verse.

metropolitan: describes a city and its surrounding area.

Middle Ages: a period in European history from about 350 to 1450 CE.

milliner: a person who designs, makes, or sells women's hats.

minority: a part of the population that is different or is a smaller group.

mob: a large and disorderly crowd of people.

moderate: not following extreme views, especially in politics.

moral: relating to right and wrong behavior and character.

mortality: the condition of being subject to death.

multicultural: made of different cultures and backgrounds.

munitions: materials used in war, especially weapons and ammunition.

Night of Terror: the brutal treatment of female suffragists at the hands of prison guards on November 14, 1917.

nonbinary: gender identities that are not exclusively masculine or feminine.

obligation: something that must be done.

oppression: an unjust or cruel use of authority and power.

oral contraceptive: taking by mouth, a pill to reduce the risk of pregnancy.

pacifist: someone who does not believe in violence or war.

pagan: someone who worships many gods or who has little or no religion.

patriarchy: a system of society or government in which men hold the power and women are largely excluded from it.

patriotic: a feeling of devotion to and love for one's country.

peasant: a farmer during the Middle Ages who lived on and farmed land owned by his lord.

perspective: a person's point of view.

philosophy: the study of truth, wisdom, the nature of reality, and knowledge.

picket: a person or group of people standing outside a place of work or other venue, protesting something or trying to persuade others.

politics: the business of governments.

polygraph: a lie detector test that measures a person's physical reactions to questions.

popular culture: the mainstream ideas, images, music, literature, movies, and other phenomenon of a particular society during a particular time.

poverty: the state of being very poor.

precedent: a decision that serves as a guide for the future.

prejudice: an unfair feeling of dislike for a person or group, usually based on gender, race, or religion.

preventive: stopping something before it happens.

privilege: a right or benefit that is given to some people but not to others.

Prohibition: a law that forbid manufacturing and selling alcohol in the United States between 1920 and 1933.

prosperity: a state of success, wealth, or comfort.

prosthetic: an artificial device that replaces a missing part of the body.

protest: to strongly object to something, often in public.

Protestant: a branch of Christianity.

Quaker: a member of the Religious Society of Friends who is devoted to peaceful principles.

queer: an inclusive term used to identify with the LGBTQ community as a whole. It may also relate to a gender or sexual orientation that does not correspond with established ideas about sexuality and gender.

race: a group of people of common ancestry who share certain physical characteristics such as skin color.

racism: to believe that all members of a race possess certain traits and to judge these traits as inferior to one's own. Negative opinions or treatment of people based on race.

radical: extreme, or a person with extreme political or social views.

rape: sexual intercourse without consent.

ratification: the action of signing or giving formal consent to a treaty, contract, or agreement, making it officially valid.

ratify: to give official approval of something, such as a constitutional amendment.

rebellion: violent resistance to authority.

refuge: a place that gives protection.

reign: the period of time a ruler rules.

Renaissance: the period of European history from the 1300s to the 1600s, which is marked by a flourishing of literature and art.

repeal: to cancel a law.

repercussion: an unintended consequence.

reproductive: having to do with producing offspring.

resistance: to fight to prevent something from happening.

resolution: a formal expression of opinion, will, or intent voted by an official body or assembled group.

revere: to honor and show respect.

revolt: to fight against a government or person of authority.

revolution: a dramatic, widespread change in society.

role: the expected behavior and characteristics of an individual.

sabotage: the planned destruction of property, or an act that interferes with work or another activity.

second-wave feminism: a period during the 1960s and '70s when feminism touched on every area of women's experience, including family, sexuality, and work.

sentinel: a soldier or guard whose job is to stand and keep watch.

sermon: a speech on a religious or moral subject.

sexism: negative opinions or treatment of people based on gender.

sexual harassment: harassment involving the making of unwanted sexual advances or obscene remarks.

sexual orientation: a person's sexual identity in relation to the gender to which they are attracted.

sexual revolution: the change in established social and moral attitudes toward sex, particularly in Western countries during the 1960s, as the women's movement and developments in contraception led to changes in attitudes toward sex and and sexual equality became an aim of society.

skepticism: doubting the truth of something.

social: living in groups.

social class: describes the level of wealth of a person in a society.

social justice: when people are treated fairly and equally within a society.

speakeasy: an illegal store or nightclub selling alcohol during Prohibition.

standoff: a deadlock between two equally matched opponents in a dispute or conflict.

statistically: based on data.

sterilization: surgery to make a person or animal unable to produce offspring.

stigma: when someone is thought less of because of who they are or what their circumstances are.

strategic: carefully designed to serve a particular purpose.

strident: loud, harsh, grating.

suburban: having to do with living areas at the edges of towns and cities.

suffrage: the right to vote.

suffrage movement: the fight to win the right to vote for women.

suffragist: a person advocating for the right of women especially and other groups to vote.

superficial: not having or showing any depth of character or understanding.

Taliban: an Islamic fundamentalist political movement in Afghanistan.

temperance: the practice of drinking little or no alcohol.

GLOSSARY

terminate: to come to an end.

testify: to give evidence as a witness in a law court.

textiles: having to do with cloth and weaving.

third-wave feminism: a period during the early 1990s through 2012 that highlighted individualism and diversity within the feminist movement.

transgender: a person whose actual gender differs from the gender they were assigned at birth.

treason: the crime of betraying one's country.

tumultuous: marked by violent or overwhelming turbulence or upheaval.

turbulent: characterized by conflict, disorder, or confusion; out of control.

tyranny: cruel and unfair treatment by people in power.

unalienable: something that cannot be taken away or denied.

unanimous: when a group is in full agreement.

unconstitutional: not in accordance with the ideals of the U.S. Constitution.

unilateral: done or undertaken by one person or party.

urban: relating to a city.

verdict: a legal decision made by a judge or jury.

veteran: a former soldier.

vilify: to speak or write about someone or something in an aggressive manner.

vindictive: disposed to seek revenge.

visibility: the state of being able to see or be seen.

white supremacy: the racist belief that white people are superior to those of all other races, and should therefore dominate society.

RESOURCES

BOOKS

Jennings, Jazz. *Being Jazz: My Life as a (Transgender) Teen.* Ember, 2017.

Sidman, Joyce. *The Girl Who Drew Butterflies: How Maria Merian's Art Changed the World.* HMH Books for Young Readers, 2018.

Thomas, Angie. *The Hate U Give.* Balzer + Bray, 2017.

Jensen, Kelly, ed. *Here We Are: Feminism for the Real World.* Algonquin Young Readers, 2017.

Fleming, Melissa. *A Hope More Powerful Than the Sea.* Flatiron Books, 2017.

Behar, Ruth. *Lucky Broken Girl.* Nancy Paulsen Books, 2017.

Yousafzai, Malala. *I Am Malala.* Little, Brown and Company, 2013.

Dias, Marley. *Marley Dias Gets It Done and So Can You.* Scholastic Press, 2018.

Charleyboy, Lisa, and Mary Beth Leatherdale, eds. *#NotYourPrincess: Voices of Native American Women.* Annick Press, 2017.

Watson, Renée. *Piecing Me Together.* Bloomsbury USA Childrens, 2017.

Spotswood, Jessica, ed. *The Radical Element: 12 Stories of Daredevils, Debutantes and Other Dauntless Girls.* Candlewick, 2018.

Schatz, Kate. *Rad Girls Can: Stories of Bold, Brave, and Brilliant Young Women (Rad Women).* Ten Speed Press, 2018.

The Girls in Science series from Nomad Press

WEBSITES

The National Women's History Museum: Explore topics and articles on women's history.
womenshistory.org/womens-history

The National Archives: Explore memorabilia from the women's movement.
archives.gov/news/topics/womens-history

MUSEUMS

National Women's History Museum
womenshistory.org

Museum of Women's Resistance
museumofwomensresistance.org

QR CODE GLOSSARY

page 4: youtube.com/watch?v=GjYtacfcgPU

page14: brooklynmuseum.org/eascfa/ dinner_party/place_settings/hypatia

page 18: nationalgeographic.com/ explore/history/salem-witch-trials

page 19: britannica.com/biography/ Eleanor-of-Aquitaine

page 27: obamawhitehouse.archives. gov/blog/find-the-sentiments

page 28: nps.gov/wori/learn/historyculture/ declaration-of-sentiments.htm

page 34: susanbanthonyhouse.org/blog/wp-content/ uploads/2017/07/Sojourner-Truth-1851.pdf

page 48: bellatory.com/fashion-industry/ WomensFashionsofthe1920- FlappersandtheJazz-Age

page 49: youtube.com/watch?v=5Bo3f_9hLkQ

page 50: npr.org/2008/11/15/96654742/a- depression-era-anthem-for-our-times

page 55: youtube.com/watch?v=ufsnk27SK9I

page 61: bbc.com/news/world-45303069

page 65: onlinemasters.ohio.edu/blog/ understanding-the-importance-of-title-ix

page 70: youtube.com/watch?v=blEevmYq1VA

page 71: youtube.com/watch?v=RTGiKYqk0gY

page 71: youtube.com/watch?v=F4D9jQpecVo

page 90: lesbianherstoryarchives.org

page 91: youtube.com/watch?v=kwjiaCRzktQ

page 92: tate.org.uk/art/artists/guerrilla- girls-6858/who-are-guerrilla-girls

page 94: npr.org/sections/ goatsandsoda/2016/07/29/487360094/ invisibilia-no-one-thought-this-all- womans-debate-team-could-crush-it

page 96: americanrhetoric.com/speeches/ hillaryclintonbeijingspeech.htm

page 106: variety.com/2018/biz/news/ emma-gonzalez-gun-violence-victims- power-of-women-1202978914

RESOURCES

SOURCE NOTES

CHAPTER 1

1 jstor.org/stable/42924397?seq=1#page_scan_tab_contents
2 thoughtco.com/women-in-1800s-4141147
3 localhistories.org/womensjobs.html
4 landofthebrave.info/colonial-women.htm
5 en.wikipedia.org/wiki/Women_in_the_workforce
6 theguardian.com/money/us-money-blog/2014/aug/11/women-rights-money-timeline-history
7 plainshumanities.unl.edu/encyclopedia/doc/egp.gen.040, https://memory.
loc.gov/ammem/awhhtml/awlaw3/property_law.html
8 britannica.com/biography/Boudicca
9 britannica.com/biography/Elizabeth-I
10 design.tutsplus.com/articles/10-influential-women-of-art-throughout-history--cms-25924
11 womenhistoryblog.com/2014/02/elizabeth-cary-agassiz.html
12 britannica.com/biography/Hypatia
13 openlibrary.org/search?isbn=081221787X&mode=everything

CHAPTER 2

1 teacher.scholastic.com/activities/suffrage/history.htm
2 Frederick Douglass, *Woman's Journal*, April 14, 1888

CHAPTER 3

1 vintagedancer.com/1920s/when-to-wear-what-in-the-1920s
2 huffpost.com/entry/1920s-hairstyles-photos_n_3720290
3 amarillo.com/news/local-news/2012-11-15/beilue-women-recall-lif…
4 en.wikipedia.org/wiki/Women_in_Bletchley_Park
5 npr.org/2010/03/09/123773525/female-wwii-pilots-the-original-fly-girls
6 history.com/news/female-allied-spy-world-war-2-wooden-leg
7 bls.gov/opub/ted/2000/feb/wk3/art03.htm

CHAPTER 4

1 leaf.tv/articles/clothing-styles-of-the-60s-70s
2 en.wikipedia.org/wiki/Mary_Quant
3 racked.com/2016/12/5/13778914/pantsuits-history
4 theatlantic.com/health/archive/2014/10/the-team-that-invented-the-birth-control-pill/380684
5 japantimes.co.jp/news/2009/10/20/reference/abortion-still-key-birth-control/#.W-X-X5NKhPY
6 britannica.com/biography/Golda-Meir
7 web.archive.org/web/20141111182057/http://www.uic.edu/orgs/
cwluherstory/jofreeman/polhistory/chisholm.htm

SOURCE NOTES (CONTINUED)

CHAPTER 5

1 en.wikipedia.org/wiki/Women%27s_liberation_movement_in_Europe

2 theguardian.com/commentisfree/2013/apr/09/margaret-thatcher-no-feminist

3 npr.org/templates/story/story.php?storyId=5447283

4 businessinsider.com/how-clarence-thomas-grew-to-hate-affirmative-action-2013-10

5 britannica.com/biography/Taslima-Nasrin

CHAPTER 6

1 combaheerivercollective.wecbly.com/the-combahee-river-collective-statement.html

2 asiasociety.org/nisha-ganatra-lesbianism-moms-and-making-chutney-popcorn

3 en.wikipedia.org/wiki/Sandy_Stone_(artist)

4 en.wikipedia.org/wiki/Feminist_views_on_transgender_topics#The_term_%22TERF%22.

5 justice.gov/opa/speech/attorney-general-loretta-e-lynch-delivers-remarks-press-conference-announcing-complaint

CHAPTER 7

1 washingtonpost.com/news/monkey-cage/wp/2017/02/07/this-is-what-we-learned-by-counting-the-womens-marches/?noredirect=on&utm_term=.85049ebaad4c

2 whitehouse.gov/briefings-statements/remarks-vice-president-pence-susan-b-anthony-list-life-issues-institute-luncheon

3 pewsocialtrends.org/2014/06/05/growing-number-of-dads-home-with-the-kids

4 athomedad.org/media-resources/statistics

5 forbes.com/sites/nealegodfrey/2017/07/31/the-stay-at-home-dad-syndrome/#385f7b581e2c

6 pewsocialtrends.org/2014/06/05/growing-number-of-dads-home-with-the-kids

INDEX

INDEX